MEZZE

MEZZE

More than 50 recipes for dips, salads & other small plates to share

RYLAND PETERS & SMALL

Designer Paul Stradling
Editor Abi Waters
Production Manager Gordana Simakovic
Creative Director Leslie Harrington
Editorial Director Julia Charles

Indexer Vanessa Bird

Published in 2025 by Ryland Peters & Small
20–21 Jockey's Fields
London WC1R 4BW
and
1452 Davis Bugg Road,
Warrenton, NC 27589

www.rylandpeters.com
email: euregulations@rylandpeters.com

Text © Valerie Aikman-Smith, Ghillie Başan, Clare Ferguson, Tori Haschka, Kathy Kordalis, Theo A. Michaels, Shelagh Ryan, Rena Salaman and Ryland Peters & Small 2025.
Design and photography © Ryland Peters & Small 2025. (See page 128 for full credits.)

ISBN: 978-1-78879-684-2

10 9 8 7 6 5 4 3 2 1

The authors' moral rights have been asserted. All rights reserved. No part of this publication may be reproduced, stored in a retrieval system or transmitted in any form or by any means, electronic, mechanical, photocopying or otherwise, without the prior permission of the publisher.

A CIP record for this book is available from the British Library.
US Library of Congress Cataloging-in-Publication data has been applied for.

The authorised representative in the EEA is Authorised Rep Compliance Ltd., Ground Floor, 71 Lower Baggot Street, Dublin, D02 P593, Ireland
www.arccompliance.com

Printed and bound in China.

NOTES

• Both British (Metric) and American (Imperial ounces plus US cups) are included in these recipes for your convenience; however, it is important to work with one set of measurements only and not alternate between the two within a recipe.

• All spoon measurements are level unless otherwise specified.

• All eggs are medium (UK) or large (US), unless specified as large, in which case US extra-large should be used. Uncooked or partially cooked eggs should not be served to the very old, frail, young children, pregnant women or those with compromised immune systems.

• Ovens should be preheated to the specified temperatures. We recommend using an oven thermometer. If using a fan-assisted oven, adjust temperatures according to the manufacturer's instructions.

• When a recipe calls for the grated zest of citrus fruit, buy unwaxed fruit and wash well before using. If you can only find treated fruit, scrub well in warm soapy water before using.

MIX
Paper | Supporting responsible forestry
FSC® C008047

CONTENTS

INTRODUCTION 7

DIPS & HOT CHEESE 8

PASTRIES, PATTIES & BREADS 32

SALADS & VEGGIE PLATES 52

FISH & SEAFOOD 82

MEAT & POULTRY 106

INDEX 126

CREDITS 128

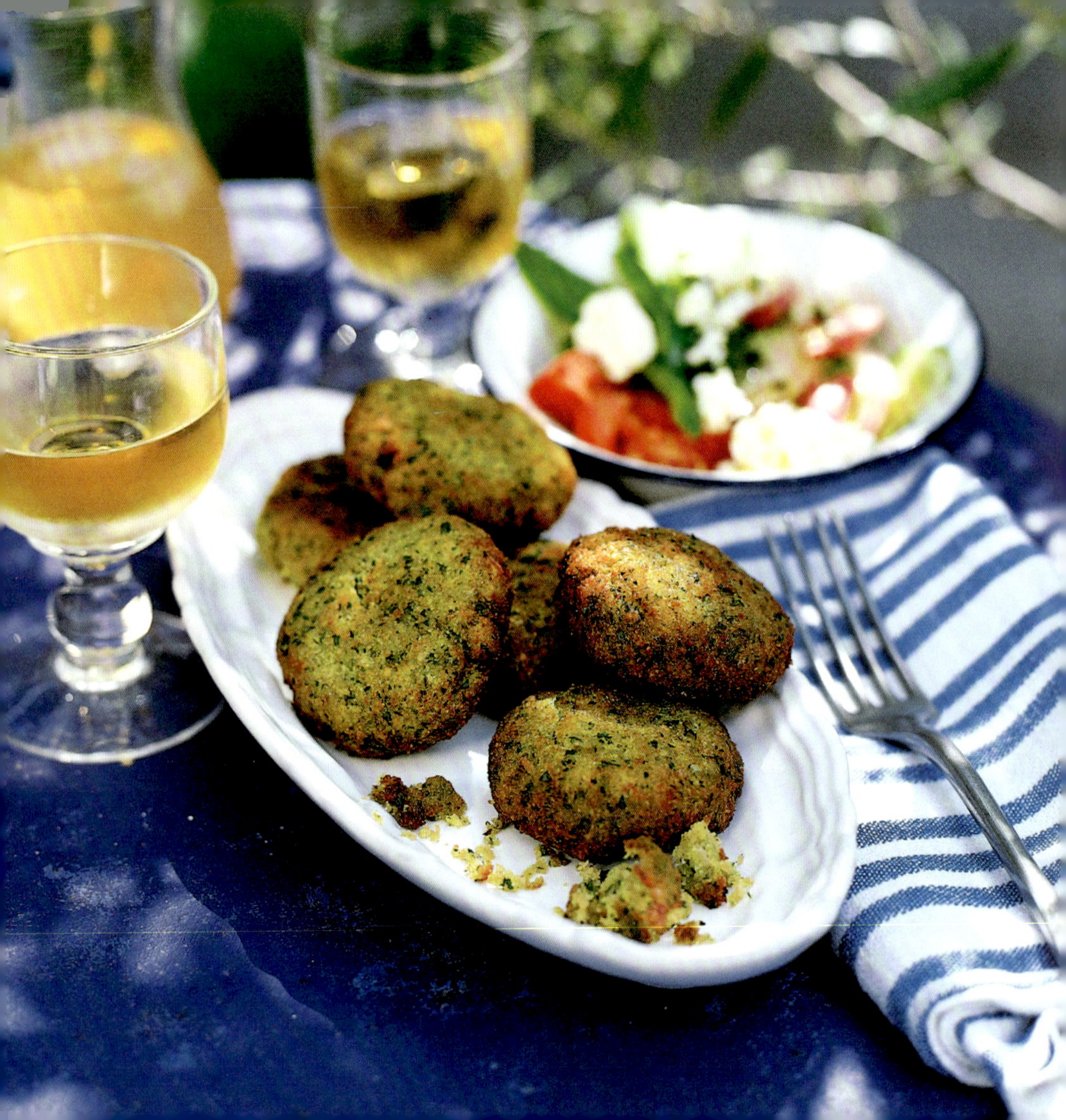

INTRODUCTION

Mention the word mezze and it instantly evokes celebration and excess. Sharing small plates with family and friends is embedded in Mediterranean culture, particularly eastern Mediterranean; however this famous cultural tradition shares many similarities with Spanish tapas and Italian antipasti. It is food to be shared – and celebrated.

The word mezze (or meze) is synonymous with celebrations, small plates and sharing, not only in Greece and Turkey, but further across the Balkans and the Middle East.

A mezze can be a simple appetizer or a complete meal. In Greece, it might be a small plate of olives, a few salted anchovies or small cubes of feta cheese sprinkled with olive oil to accompany an evening ouzo.

However, mezze evolves and changes to fit the occasion. The more important the occasion or the guests, the more intricate the dishes. At its most elaborate, as with Lebanese mezze, it can be a glorious banquet, including hummus, tabbouleh, delicate little pastries, kibbeh, sizzling kebabs/kabobs and golden falafels.

In this book, you'll find all the recipes you need to put together perfect platters and generous grazing boards packed full of dips and dippers, bite-size pastries, homemade breads, fresh fish, meaty skewers and a plethora of other tasty morsels inspired by Greek, Turkish and Middle Eastern cuisines.

These regions are blessed with bountiful fresh produce and they make the most of them in an array of salads and vegetable dishes, so there is plenty on offer for vegetarians – from grilled aubergines/eggplants and roasted peppers to those famous stuffed vine leaves.

Whether you're serving a few nibbles or a sharing banquet, there is plenty of inspiration to be found here – a mezze feast awaits!

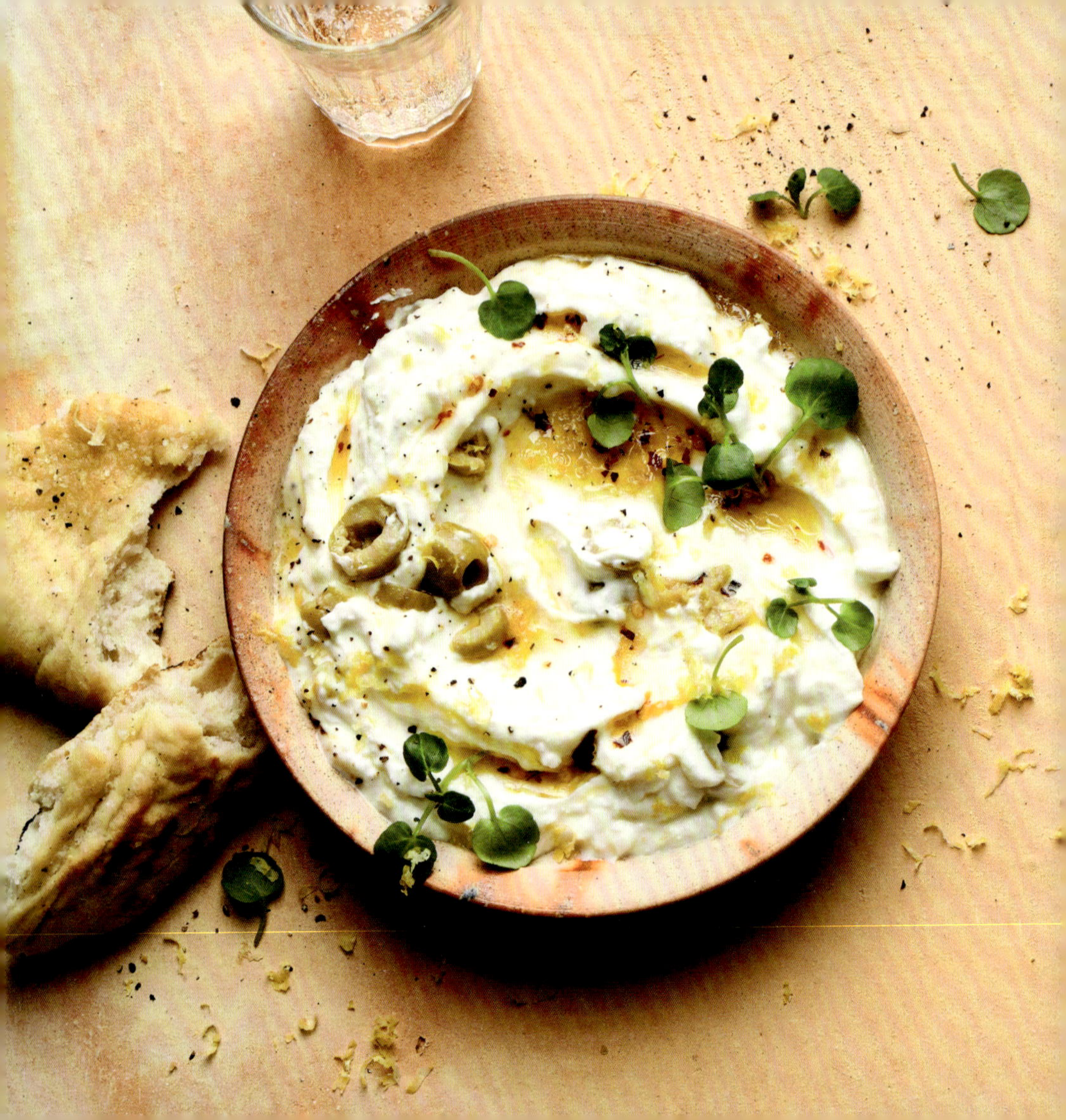

1
DIPS & HOT CHEESE

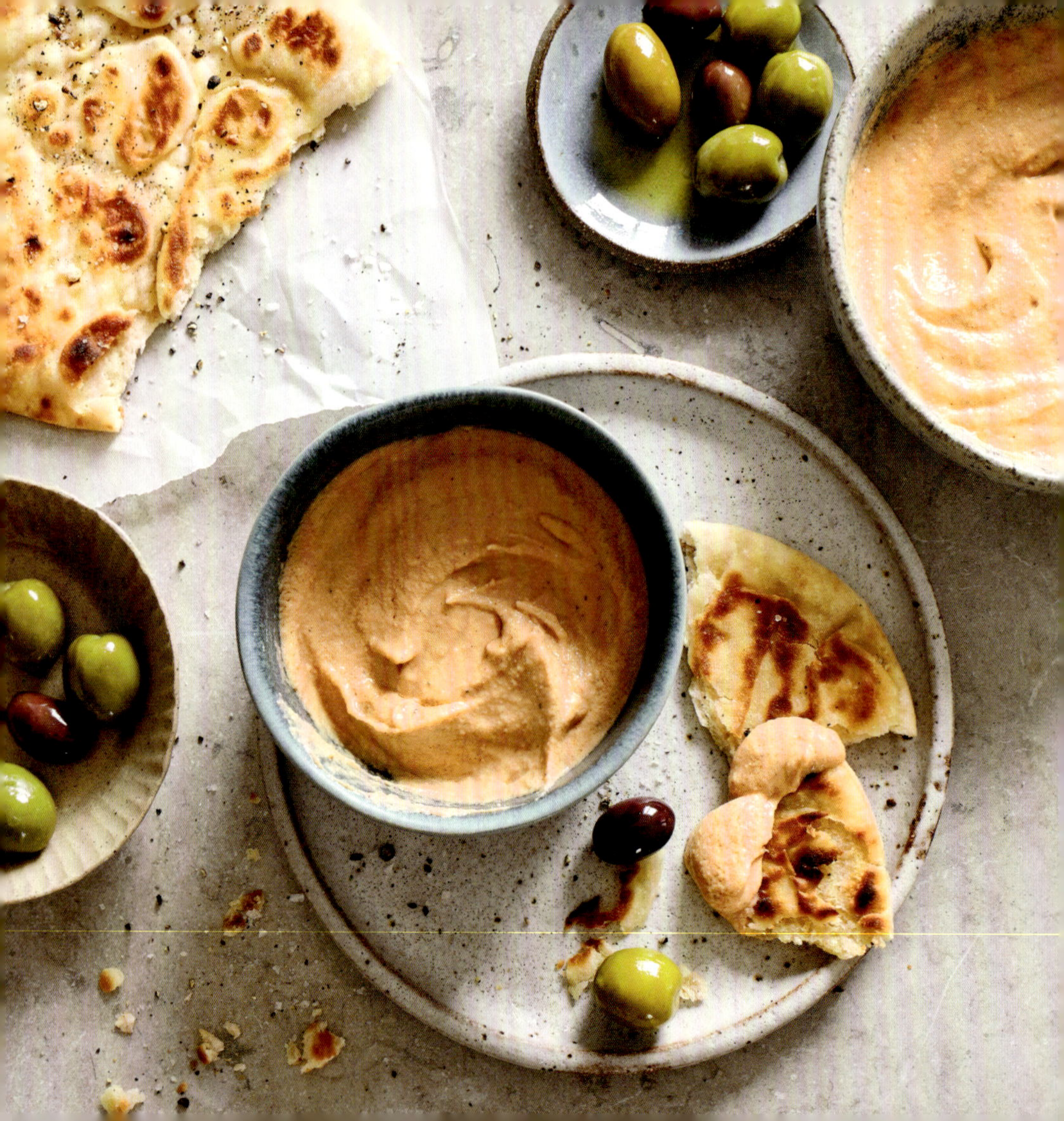

TARAMASALATA

200-g/7-oz. can cod roe, drained

1 small red onion, grated (about 20 g/2 tbsp)

½ tsp cayenne pepper

2 tbsp freshly squeezed lemon juice

1 chunky slice of toasted bread (about 50 g/2 oz.)

50 ml/3½ tbsp milk

100 ml/scant ½ cup extra virgin olive oil, plus extra to serve

salt and black pepper

TO SERVE
olives

toasted pitta bread

MAKES ABOUT 500 G/ 2 CUPS

Homemade taramasalata is a world away from supermarket pots. Add this traditional cod roe dip to a mezze selection or simply devour it with some toasted pitta breads and a few olives.

Add the drained cod roe to a food processor, breaking it up with the back of a fork, then add the grated onion, cayenne pepper and lemon juice, and season generously with salt and black pepper.

Soak the toasted bread in the milk for a minute, then squeeze out the excess liquid and tear the toast into the food processor (discard the leftover milk). Pulse everything in the food processor to begin with, then increase the speed and start drizzling in the olive oil until it has all been added.

Depending on consistency, you can add a few tablespoons of water at the end to smooth the taramasalata. Taste, adding more salt, lemon juice or cayenne as preferred.

Serve in a bowl with a little extra drizzle of olive oil, a few olives alongside and some toasted pitta bread for dipping.

ROASTED RED PEPPER & CHICKPEA HUMMUS

50 g/2 oz. roasted red (bell) peppers from a jar or can

400-g/14-oz. can chickpeas/garbanzo beans, drained (reserve a splash of the liquid)

3 tbsp extra virgin olive oil

1 garlic clove, lightly crushed

2 tsp freshly squeezed lemon juice

½ fresh red chilli/chile (optional)

½ tsp salt

TO SERVE

crumbled feta (optional)

basil leaves (optional)

MAKES ABOUT 500 G/ 2 CUPS

This delightfully simple hummus is perfect as it comes, but is even better with a bit of tangy feta cheese crumbled over the top.

Add all the ingredients to a food processor (including a splash of chickpea liquid) and blitz until you have a smooth paste. Taste for seasoning, adding more lemon juice if preferred.

Transfer to a serving bowl. If you wish, sprinkle a little crumbled feta and a few basil leaves over the top.

DIPS & HOT CHEESE

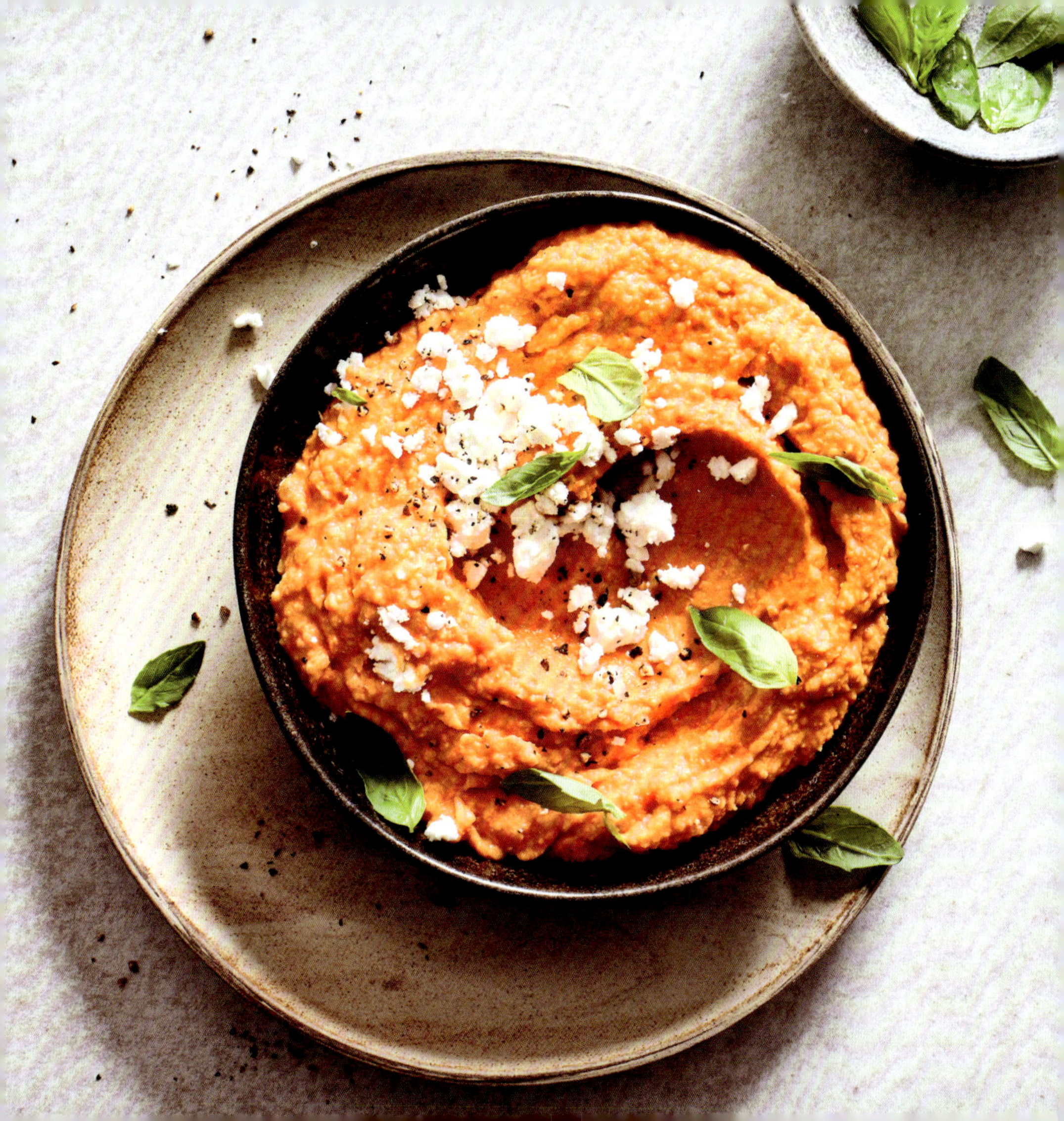

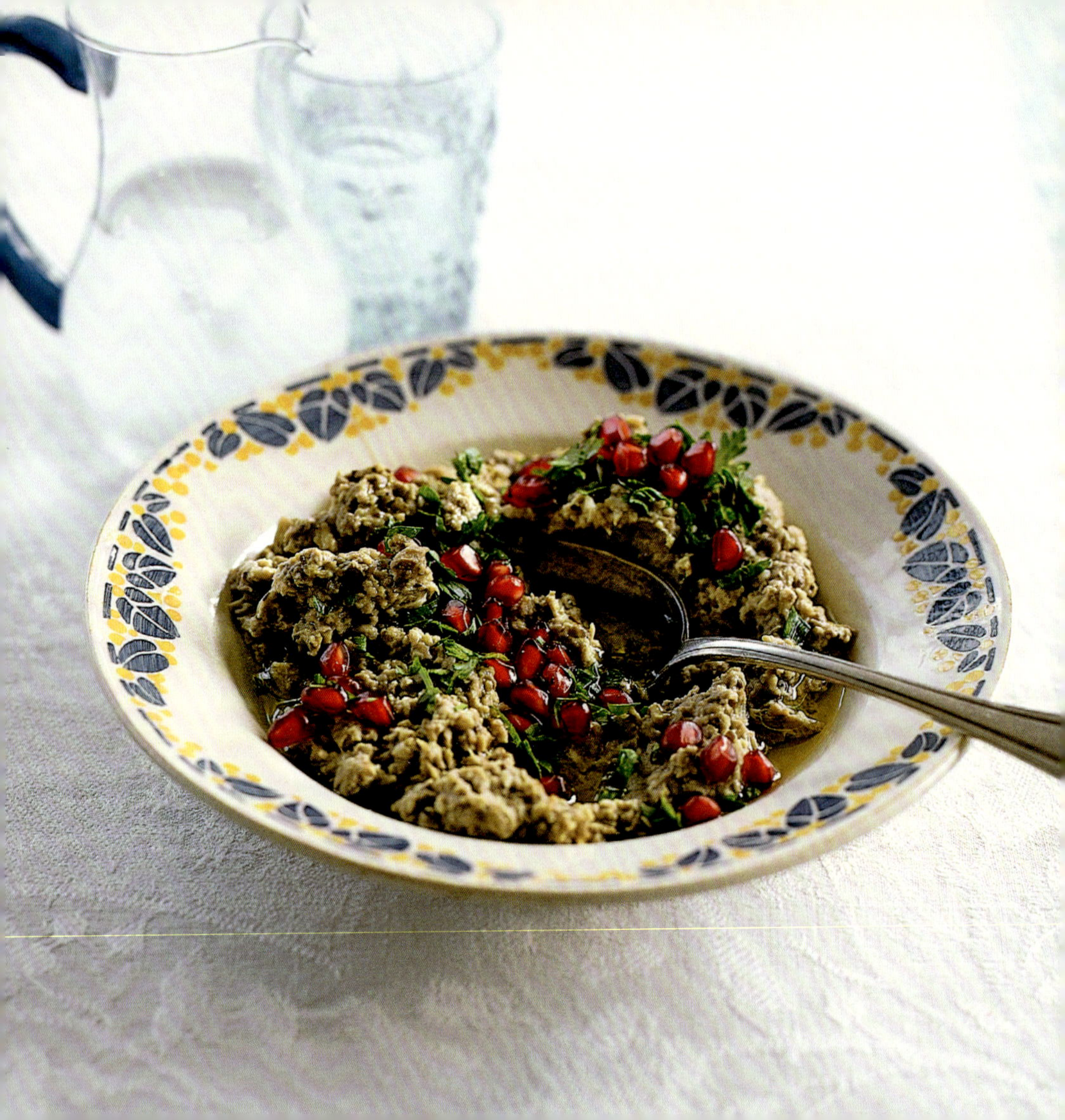

BABA GHANOUSH

The aubergine/eggplant is one of the most important participants in the mezze table. Here it is made into baba ghanoush, a Middle Eastern classic, which is rich and utterly seductive.

3 large aubergines/eggplants (about 900 g/2 lb.), rinsed and dried

2 tbsp tahini paste

2 garlic cloves, crushed

freshly squeezed juice of 1 lemon

salt and black pepper

TO SERVE

extra virgin olive oil

finely chopped flat-leaf parsley

pomegranate seeds

SERVES 6

Preheat the oven to 180°C (350°F) Gas 4.

Prick the whole aubergines with a fork to stop them exploding and put them directly on the oven shelves. Roast in the preheated oven for just under 1 hour, turning them over occasionally.

The trick after this is to remove them from the oven and lay them directly on a gentle gas flame for 2–3 minutes. Using oven gloves, hold them by their stalks and keep turning them over as they are scorched. This is quite a tricky business, but it will give you that inimitable smoky taste.

Remove from the heat and let the aubergines cool enough to handle, then slit them open and spoon the flesh into a colander to drain. Press lightly to extract the juices. Transfer the aubergine flesh to a food processor with the remaining ingredients and pulse briefly to form a coarse paste. Taste and add salt and pepper as necessary.

Spread on a platter, drizzle a tablespoon of olive oil in a decorative pattern, sprinkle some parsley and pomegranate seeds on top, and serve.

TARATOR

In Lebanon, tarator is as ubiquitous as tzatziki is in Greece. It is traditionally served with fish, but can also be thinned down and used as a salad dressing, if you like.

5 tbsp tahini paste

1 tsp ground cumin

100 ml/scant ½ cup warm water

2 garlic cloves, crushed

freshly squeezed juice of 1½ lemons

3 tbsp finely chopped flat-leaf parsley

salt

SERVES 6

If the tahini paste has separated in the jar, mix it properly with a spoon. Put the tahini in a food processor, add the cumin, water, garlic, salt and half the lemon juice and process until smooth and amalgamated – it should have the consistency of thick double/heavy cream.

Taste and adjust by adding as much lemon juice as you like. I love sharp lemony tastes, but it is a matter of personal preference.

Transfer to a bowl, stir in the parsley and serve.

TZATZIKI

This refreshing dip is an ideal partner for barbecued meats or vegetables.

200 g/6½ oz. Greek yogurt

12-cm/5-inch piece of cucumber, peeled and thickly grated

1 garlic clove, crushed

1 tbsp extra virgin olive oil

½ tsp red wine vinegar

1 tbsp finely chopped mint

salt

SERVES 6

Put the yogurt in a bowl and add the grated cucumber. Add the garlic, olive oil, vinegar, mint and salt. Mix well with a fork. Cover with clingfilm/plastic wrap and chill lightly.

Note Delicious accompaniments for tzatziki include grilled or fried vegetables. To make them, thinly slice 2 courgettes/zucchini lengthways and 2 aubergines/eggplants crossways. Pour 2.5 cm/1 inch depth of sunflower or groundnut oil into a frying pan/skillet and heat until a haze forms. Working in batches, dredge the sliced vegetables in plain/all-purpose flour, then fry in the hot oil on both sides. Remove and drain on paper towels.

DIPS & HOT CHEESE

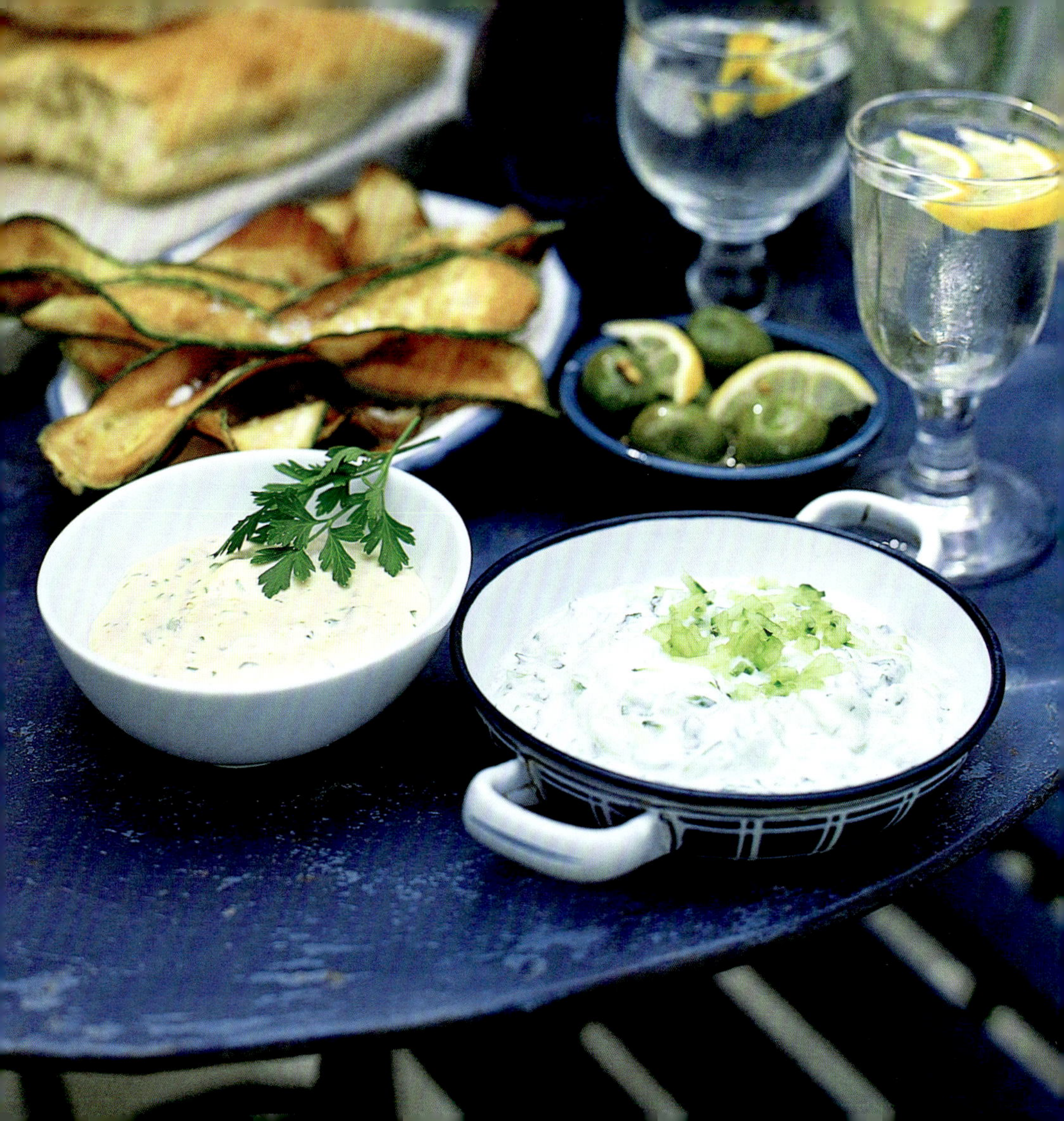

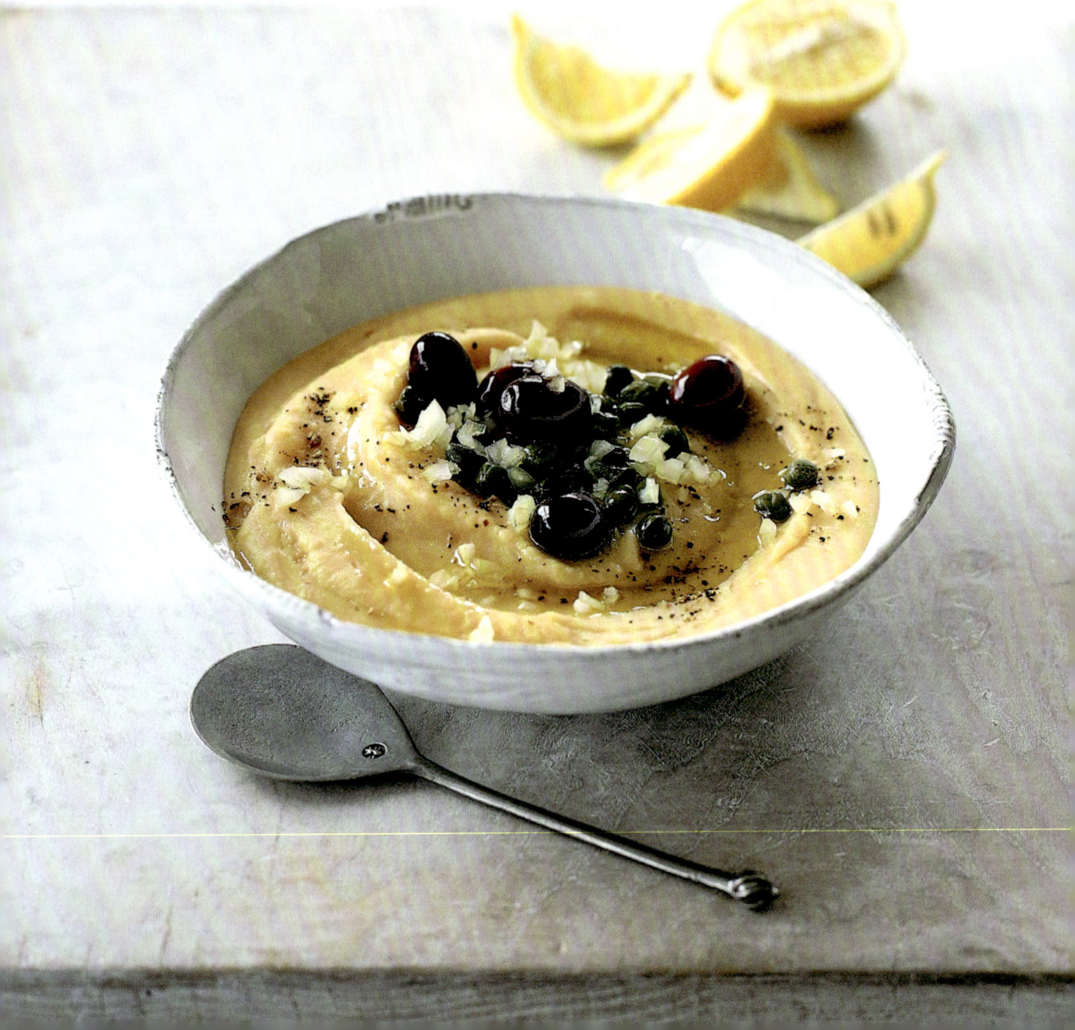

FAVA

Fava is always part of mezze in Greece. Although quite frugal, it is one of the first plates to arrive on the table, even at high-end restaurants. This dish has been on the Greek menu for several thousand years, so it really is a classic! Authentic Greek fava (the best come from the island of Santorini) may look similar to yellow split peas, but they have a much sweeter taste.

300 g/10 oz. Greek fava or yellow split peas

2 onions, finely chopped

2 tbsp capers, rinsed

5–6 tbsp extra virgin olive oil

freshly squeezed juice of 1 lemon

4–6 stoned/pitted black olives

salt and black pepper

SERVES 6

Soak the fava or split peas in cold water for 1–2 hours. Drain, rinse, put in a saucepan and cover with 2 litres/quarts water. Bring to the boil and skim until clear.

Add just over half the chopped onion and simmer, uncovered, for at least 1 hour, or until perfectly soft. Stir occasionally and add some hot water if needed. At the end of cooking, when the dish has the consistency of thick soup, add salt.

Transfer to a food processor or blender while it is still hot, process until smooth, then pour onto a large platter immediately as it solidifies when cold.

Sprinkle the capers, black pepper and the remaining chopped onion over the top, then drizzle with the olive oil and lemon juice. Pile the olives in the middle and serve warm or at room temperature.

ZHUG

8 dried red chillies/chiles

4 garlic cloves, roughly chopped

1 tsp salt

seeds of 4–6 cardamom pods

1 tsp caraway seeds

½ tsp black peppercorns

a small bunch of flat-leaf parsley, finely chopped, plus extra to garnish

a small bunch of coriander/cilantro, finely chopped, plus extra to garnish

3–4 tbsp olive oil or sunflower oil

large sterilized glass jar

MAKES 4–5 TBSP

Fiery and versatile like harissa, zhug (or zhoug) is a popular chilli paste in Yemen, Oman, the United Arab Emirates, Saudi Arabia and Egypt. Zhug is served with grilled and fried vegetables or shellfish, or is served as part of a mezze spread with chunks of fresh bread to dip into it.

Put the chillies in a bowl, pour boiling water over them and leave them to soak for at least 6 hours. Drain them, cut off the stalks, squeeze out the seeds and roughly chop them.

Using a pestle and mortar, pound the chillies with the garlic and salt to a thick, smooth paste. Add the cardamom and caraway seeds and the peppercorns, and pound them with the chilli paste – you want to break up the seeds and peppercorns, but they don't have to be perfectly ground as a little bit of texture is good. Beat in the parsley and coriander, and bind the mixture with the oil.

Spoon the spice paste into a sterilized jar, drizzle the rest of the oil over the top and keep it in a cool place, or in the refrigerator, for up to 4 weeks. When serving as a condiment or a dip for bread, mix the layer of oil into it and garnish with extra finely chopped coriander and/or parsley.

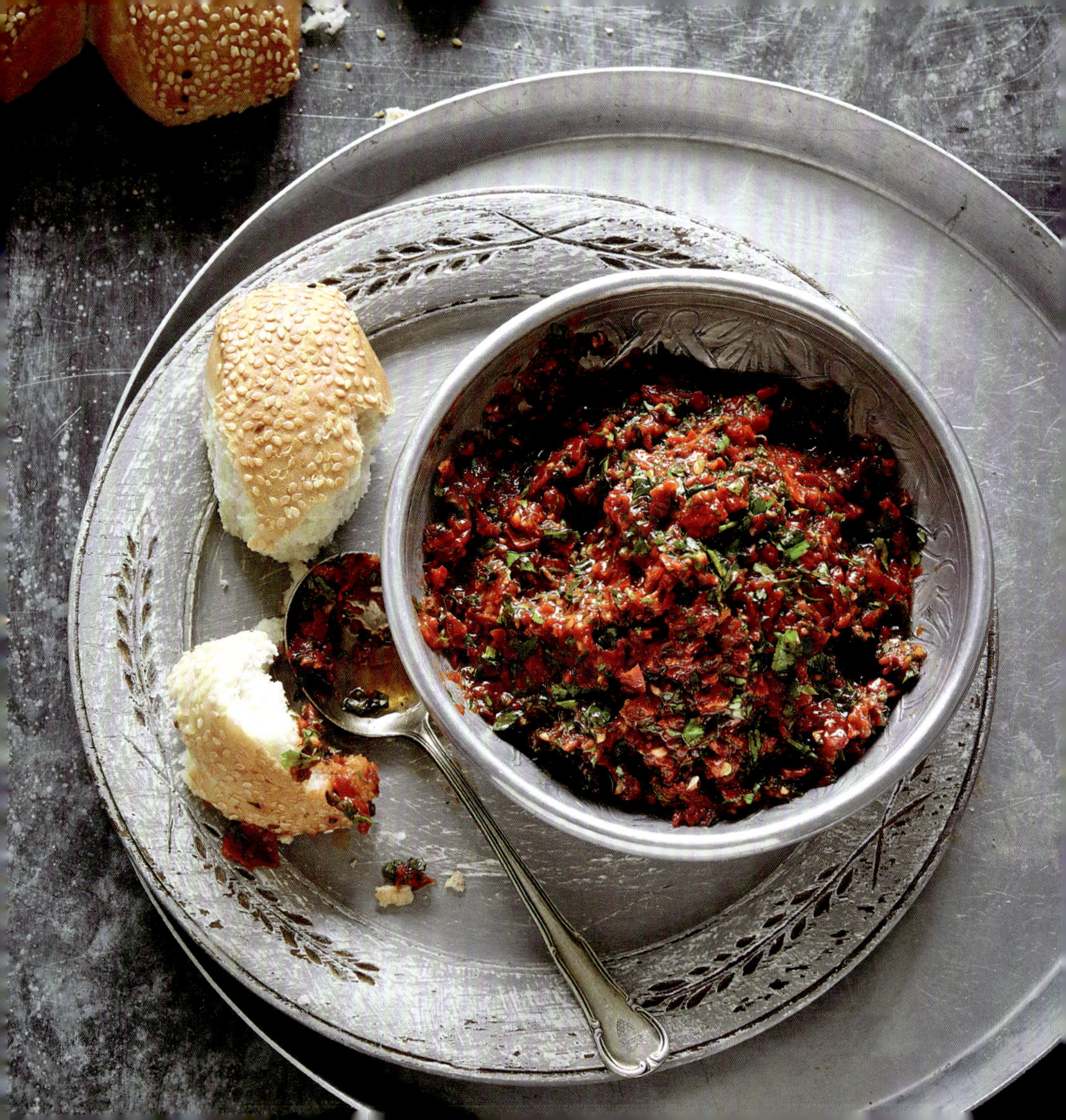

FETA & CHILLI DIP (TYROHTIPITI) *(see page 1 for image)*

2 fresh green chillies/chiles

1 large red or green (bell) pepper

250 g/9 oz. feta, thickly sliced

4 tbsp extra virgin olive oil

freshly squeezed juice of 1 small lemon

3–4 tbsp milk

1 tsp dried chilli/hot red pepper flakes

1 tbsp finely chopped flat-leaf parsley

black pepper

TO SERVE

toasted bread or crudités

metal skewer

SERVES 6

Htipiti means 'beaten' and *tyri* means 'cheese', so *tyrohtipiti* means 'beaten cheese'. This dip originated in the beautiful city of Thessaloniki, but is fast becoming popular all over Greece. Its appearance varies according to the type of peppers used and the heat of the chillies, so it can range from pink and red to green.

Thread the chillies on a metal skewer and place them over a low gas flame or on a preheated barbecue/grill. Keep turning them until scorched. Put the pepper over the flame and do the same until it feels soft and partially scorched. The pepper will take longer than the chillies. Set aside until cool enough to handle.

Deseed and peel the pepper and do the same with the chillies, which will be a little more difficult. Wipe off any blackened bits with paper towels. (Beware of the hot chillies.)

Put the chillies, pepper, feta, olive oil, lemon juice, 3 tablespoons milk and some black pepper in a food processor and blend until creamy. If too stiff, add a little more milk. Remove to a plate or bowl, sprinkle the chilli flakes and parsley on top and chill lightly.

Serve with toast or crudités.

CREAMY BUTTER BEAN DIP

400-g/14-oz. jar or can butter/lima beans (235 g/ 1½ cups drained)

60 ml/¼ cup olive oil, plus extra to serve

1 garlic clove, crushed

freshly squeezed juice of ½ lemon

½ tsp salt

2 tbsp finely chopped flat-leaf parsley

TO SERVE

1 preserved lemon, finely diced

dried chilli/hot red pepper flakes

dried oregano

SERVES 6

This delicious garlicky dip makes a great alternative to hummus and is quick and easy to make. Use the best quality butter beans you can find – the ones you buy in a jar rather than in a can have a more velvety texture, which is what we want here, but canned work too.

Add the butter beans, olive oil, garlic, lemon juice, salt and 1 tablespoon water to a food processor and blend until almost smooth – a little coarseness is quite nice. (If you prefer, put the ingredients in a bowl and use a hand-held stick blender to do this.)

Once blended, add the chopped parsley and fold it in by hand. Taste and adjust the seasoning if necessary.

Serve topped with the preserved lemon pieces, a sprinkle of dried chilli flakes and dried oregano, and finish with an extra drizzle of olive oil.

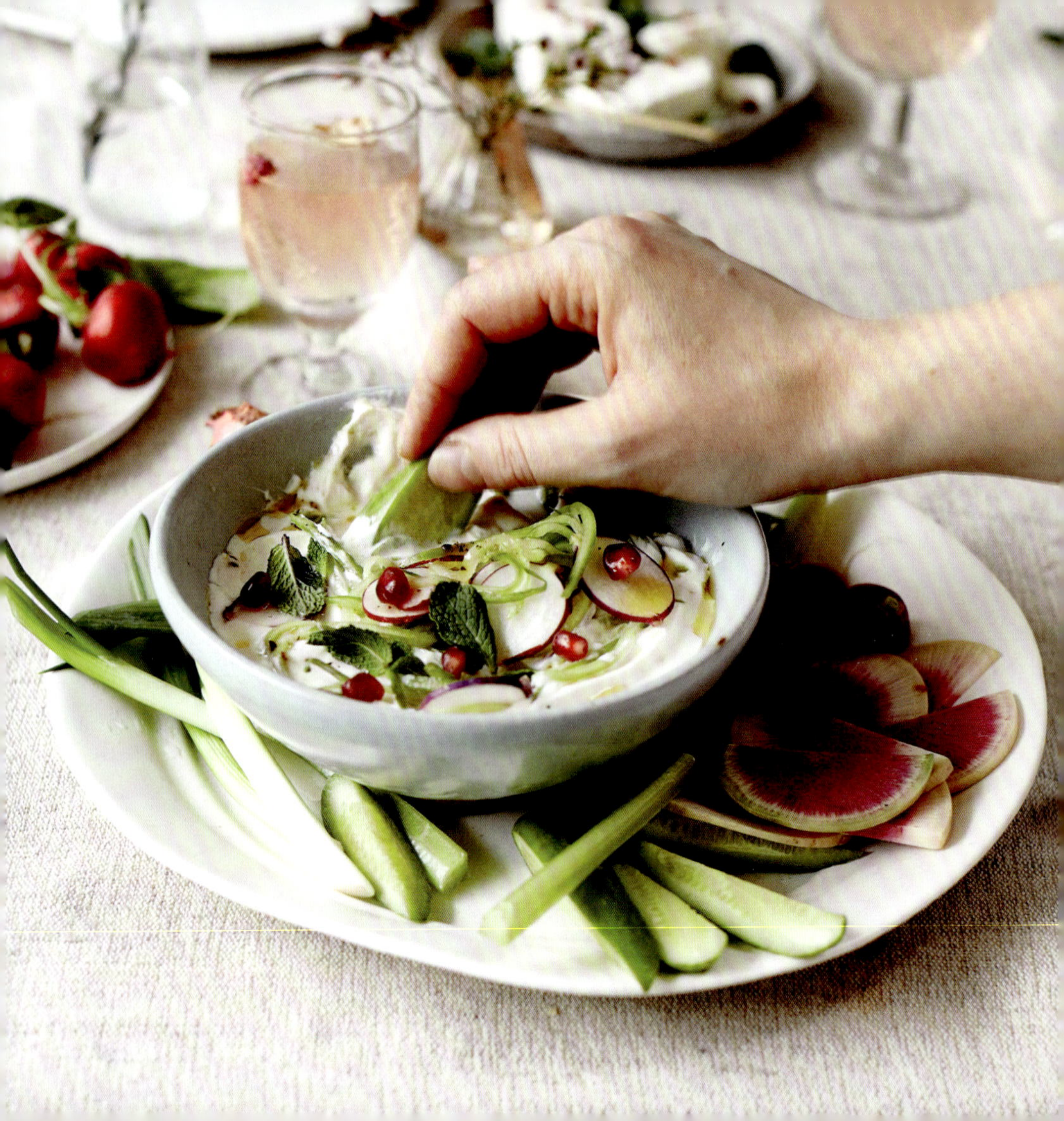

RADISH TZATZIKI

1 cucumber

5 radishes, thinly sliced

500 g/2¼ cups Greek yogurt

1 garlic clove, crushed

freshly squeezed juice of ½ lemon

3 sprigs of mint, leaves picked and chopped, plus a few leaves to garnish

1 tbsp olive oil

salt

TO SERVE

pomegranate seeds (optional)

crudités

SERVES 4–6

This twist on the classic tzatziki recipe will add a different dimension and extra crunch to any mezze meal. The crisp cucumber and radish marry perfectly with the creamy Greek yogurt.

Coarsely grate the cucumber and set some aside for the garnish. Sprinkle with a pinch of salt and squeeze out all the liquid. Tip into a bowl.

Set aside a few radish slices for the garnish, then add the rest to the bowl, along with the yogurt, garlic, lemon juice, chopped mint and olive oil. Mix well.

To serve, top with the reserved cucumber and radishes, extra mint leaves and a few pomegranate seeds. Serve with a selection of crudités.

WHIPPED SPICY HONEY FETA

WHIPPED FETA

200 g/7 oz. feta

100 g/3½ oz. ricotta

2 tbsp Greek yogurt

salt and black pepper

SPICY HONEY

2 tbsp olive oil

1 garlic clove, left whole and bruised

3 tbsp runny honey

2 tbsp freshly squeezed lemon juice

1 tsp dried chilli/hot red pepper flakes, plus extra to serve

TO SERVE

chopped green olives

pea shoots and mini cress

grated lemon zest

Yogurt Pitta (see page 51)

SERVES 4–6

Here's a huge flavour punch in just one bowl. Simply serve this mezze with the quick pittas on page 51 for a snack or a side.

Place the feta, ricotta and yogurt in a food processor, season with salt and pepper, and blend on high for 2–3 minutes until smooth. Taste and add more salt and pepper if needed.

To make the spicy honey, heat the olive oil in a saucepan over a very low heat. Add the bruised garlic and simmer gently, then turn off the heat. Stir in the honey, lemon juice and chilli flakes, and season with salt and pepper.

Serve the whipped feta in a bowl, drizzled with the spicy honey and topped with olives, pea shoots and cress, lemon zest and some extra black pepper and chilli flakes. Serve with yogurt pittas for dipping.

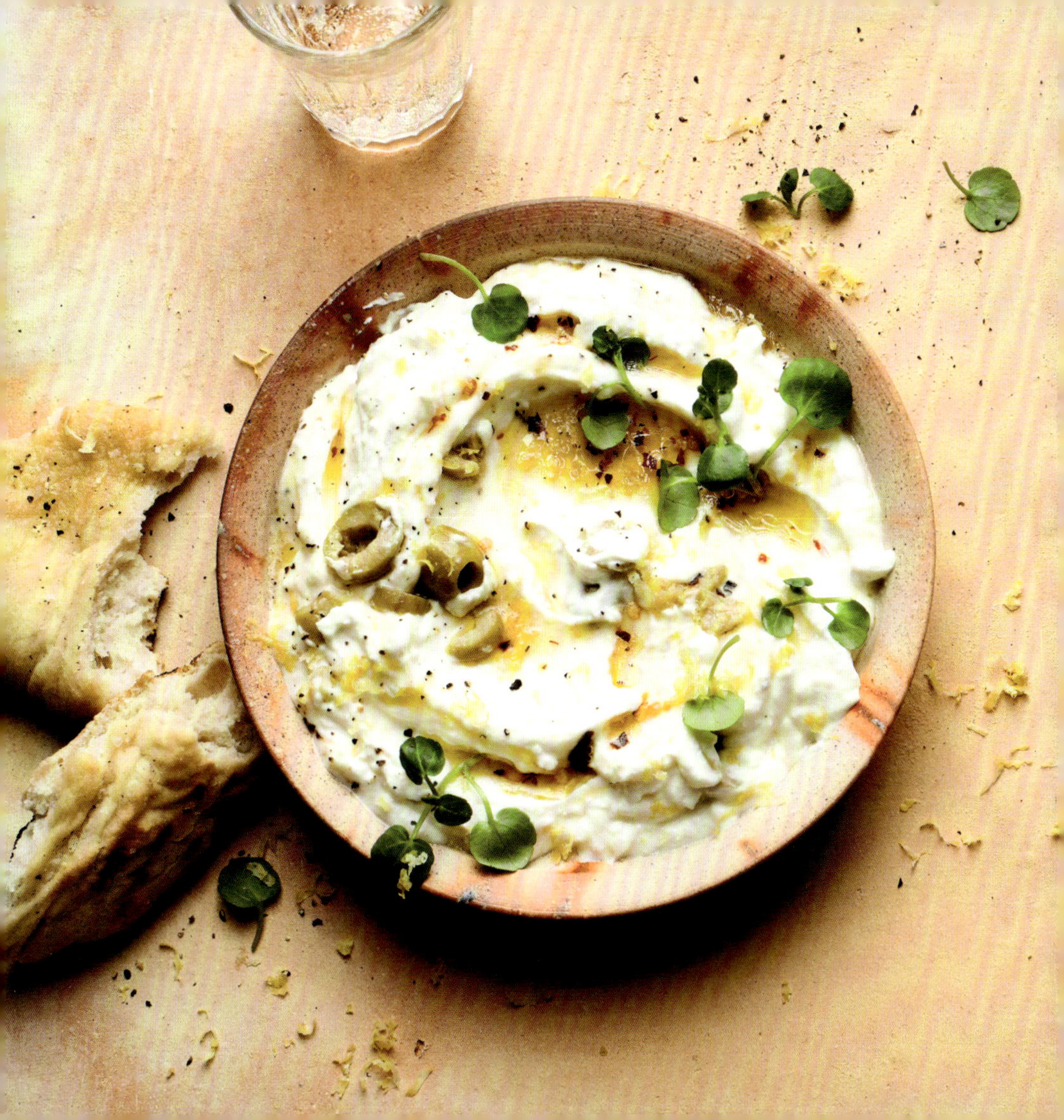

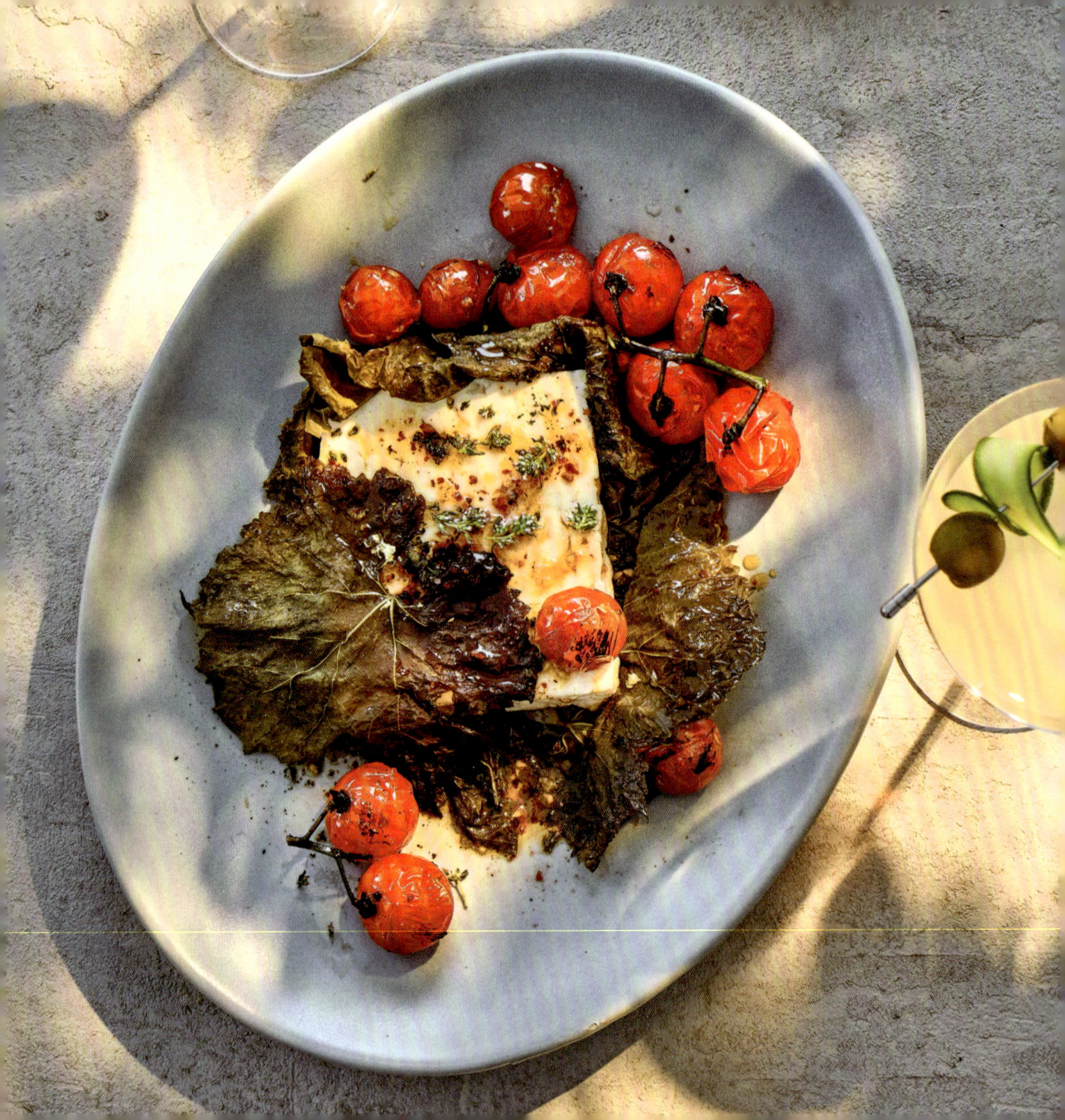

FETA BAKED IN VINE LEAVES
WITH BLISTERED TOMATOES

This is inspired by the snacks (or *mezedes*) that are served alongside an ouzo in an *ouzeri*, a drinks and snacks taverna. The baked feta is semi-wrapped in vine leaves and served with blistered tomatoes. Simply take to the table with some forks and share with all.

150 g/5 oz. cherry tomatoes on the vine

1 tsp dried chilli/hot red pepper flakes

2 tbsp extra virgin olive oil, plus extra for brushing

8 vine leaves preserved in brine, stems removed, rinsed

200-g/7-oz. block of feta, cut into 4 thick slices

grated zest of 1 lemon

1 tbsp runny honey

baking sheet, lined

SERVES 4–6

Preheat the oven to 200°C (400°C) Gas 6.

Trim the tomatoes into bunches of 3 or 4, place them on a small baking sheet and sprinkle with chilli flakes. Drizzle with the oil, season to taste and roast for 10–15 minutes until cooked through and the skin blisters.

Meanwhile, lay 2 vine leaves slightly overlapping on a work surface, brush with a little oil, place a piece of feta on top, sprinkle with lemon zest and drizzle with honey. Loosely wrap the vine leaves around the feta to form a parcel and place on the lined baking sheet. Repeat with the other feta slices and vine leaves.

Brush the parcels with oil and bake in the oven for 10–15 minutes until the feta is soft and warmed through. Serve hot with the blistered tomatoes.

SAGANAKI

This fried cheese takes its name from the small double-handled pan in which it is usually served sizzling, either in tavernas or at home. Traditionally, Greek kefalotyri cheese, which is quite salty and full of flavour, is used for this mezze dish. Cypriot halloumi also makes an appetizing alternative. If these aren't available, however, you can basically fry any strong-tasting cheese that will not melt in the process.

12 slices of kefalotyri, kasseri or halloumi, about 1 cm/½ inch thick

3 tbsp plain/all-purpose flour

3–4 tbsp light olive or groundnut oil

TO SERVE

black pepper

lemon wedges

SERVES 6

Coat each slice of cheese lightly in flour and shake off any excess. Heat half the olive oil in a non-stick frying pan/skillet and put half the slices in a single layer. Leave them for a couple of minutes and then turn them over as their edges get crisp and golden. Let them lightly brown on the other side, about 1 minute, then place them on a double layer of paper towels in order to get rid of excess oil.

Heat a little more oil in the frying pan/skillet and, when hot, repeat as before with the remaining cheese.

Serve immediately topped with a little black pepper and surrounded by lemon wedges.

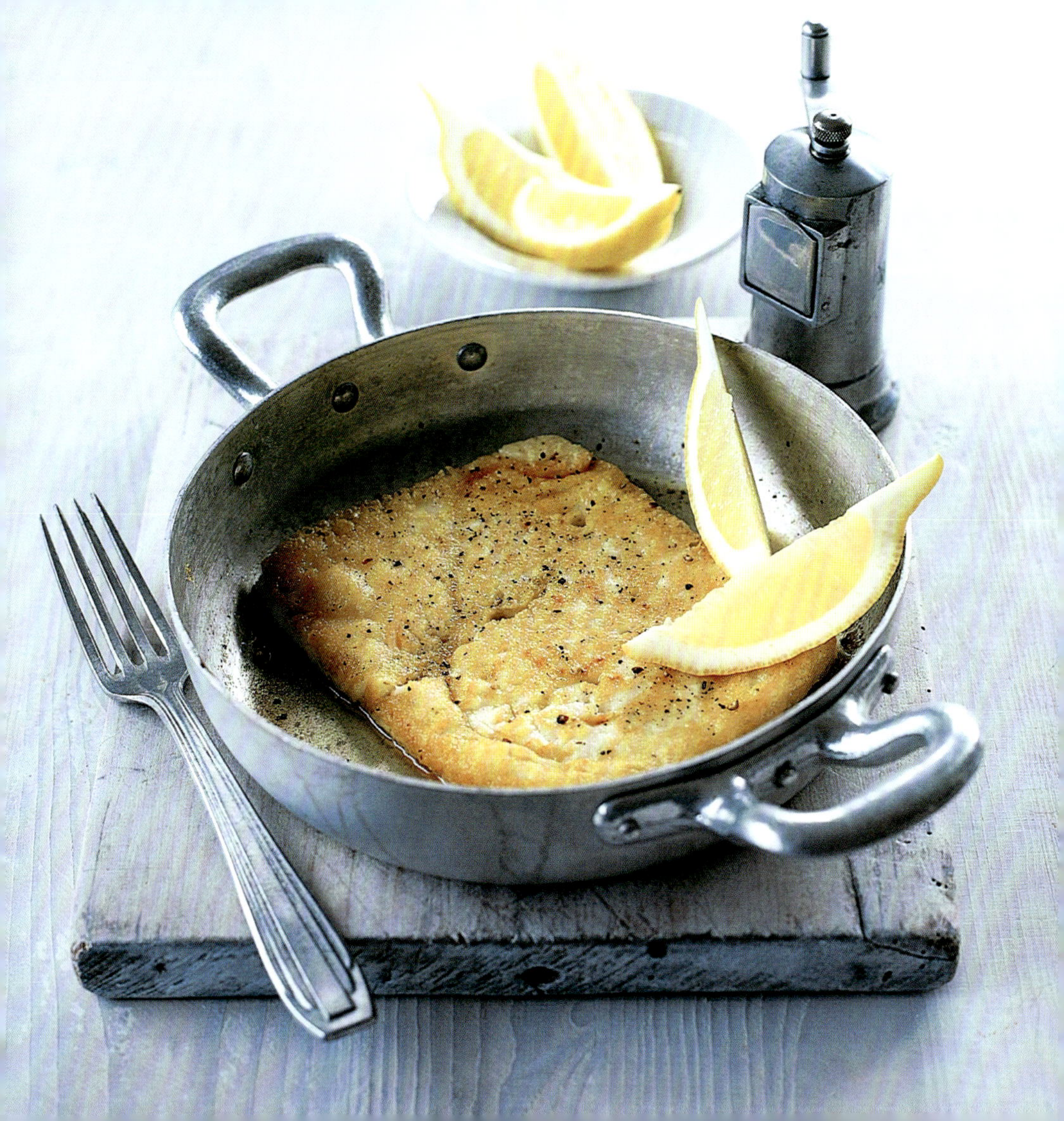

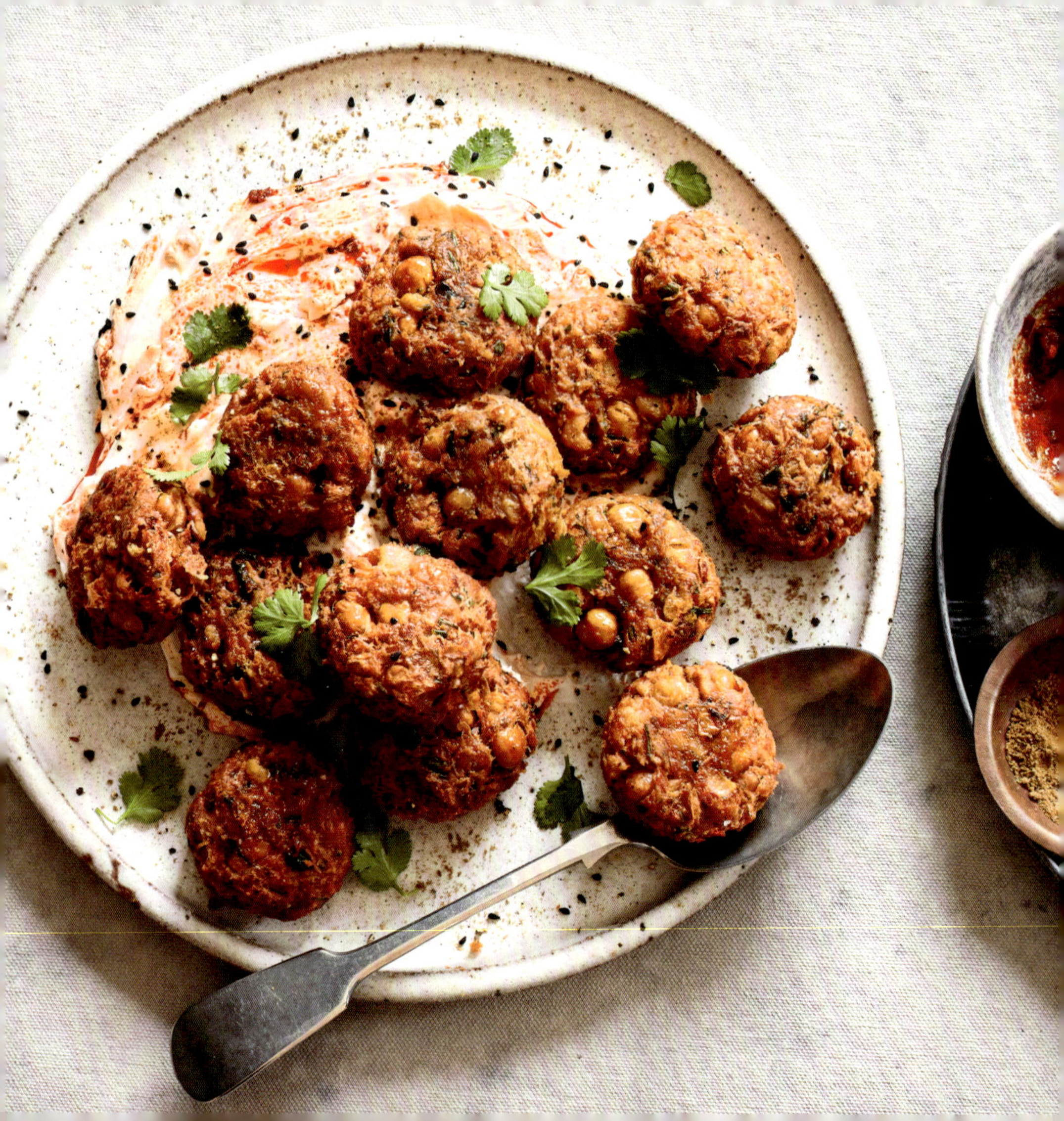

2
PASTRIES, PATTIES & BREADS

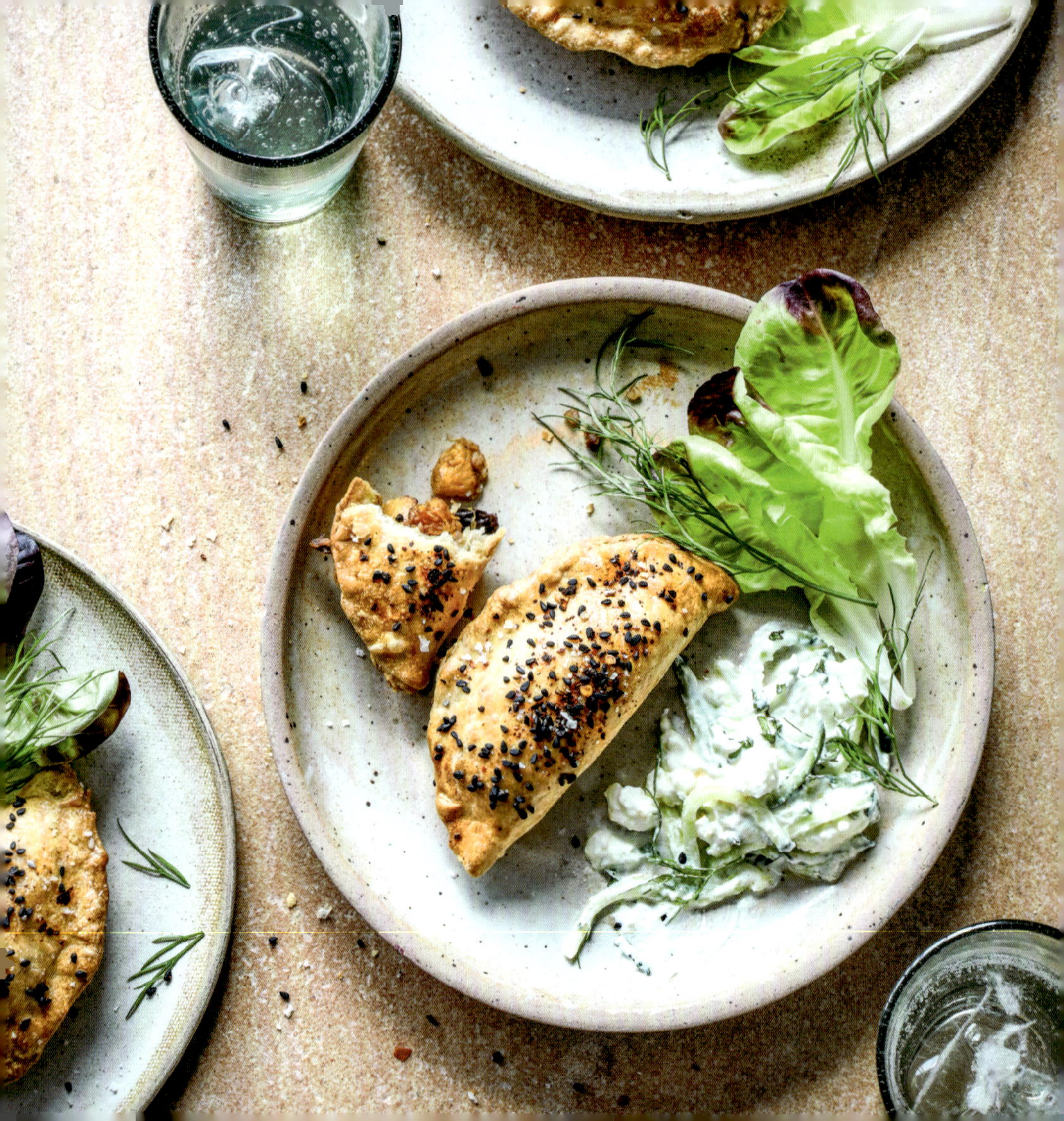

SPICED BUTTERNUT PIES

500 g/1 lb. 2 oz. butternut squash

30 g/1 oz. white onion, finely chopped

a pinch of ground cloves

a pinch of ground cumin

a generous pinch of ground cinnamon

olive oil, for drizzling

40 g/scant ¼ cup bulgur wheat

40 g/scant ⅓ cup dried cherries, chopped

400 g/14 oz. ready-made shortcrust pastry

plain/all-purpose flour, for dusting

1 egg, beaten with a splash of milk

1 tbsp nigella seeds

1 tbsp dried chilli/hot red pepper flakes

a pinch of sea salt flakes

TO SERVE
Tzatziki (see page 16)

baking sheet, lined

MAKES 8

These pies contain roasted squash, mixed with warming spices and sweet dried cherries.

Preheat the oven to 200°C (400°F) Gas 6.

To make the filling, peel the squash and cut it into 1-cm/ ½-inch cubes. Put the squash cubes and onion on a baking sheet with all the spices. Drizzle with olive oil and toss with your hands to coat the vegetables with oil and seasoning. Cook in the preheated oven for about 20 minutes, or until the squash is fork-tender, the remove from the oven. Reduce the oven temperature to 180°C (350°F) Gas 4.

Put the bulgur wheat in a heatproof mixing bowl and pour in just enough boiling water to cover. Place a plate on top and leave the grains to hydrate and fluff up. Once the bulgur has absorbed all the water, tip the cooked squash into the same bowl and add the dried cherries. Mix until combined.

Divide the shortcrust pastry into eight pieces of roughly the same size and roll each one out on a lightly floured surface, until each one is about 12 cm/5 inches in diameter.

Put 1–2 heaped tablespoons of filling on each disc, fold the pastry over and pinch along the edges to seal it in. Brush the egg and milk over the pastry to glaze, then scatter a pinch of nigella seeds, chilli flakes and sea salt over the top of each.

Place on the lined baking sheet and bake in the preheated oven for 30 minutes until golden. Serve warm with tzatziki.

PASTRIES, PATTIES & BREADS

SPINACH & CHEESE PIE (SPANAKOTYROPITTA)

400-g/16-oz. packet of filo/Phyllo pastry, thawed if frozen

150 g/9 tbsp butter, melted

FILLING

500 g/1 lb. 2 oz. spinach, rinsed

4 tbsp extra virgin olive oil

1 large onion, finely chopped

4–5 spring onions/scallions, trimmed and coarsely chopped

4 eggs

250 g/9 oz. feta

90 g/3 oz. dill, finely chopped

3–4 tbsp finely chopped flat-leaf parsley

4 tbsp milk

salt and black pepper

roasting pan (about 35 x 30 cm/13 x 9 inches)

SERVES 12

Pastries are at the heart of Greek food and culture and each village and every island has its own version that showcase local produce. This sensational pie is the most common and one of the most delicious.

Preheat the oven to 190°C (375°F) Gas 5.

To make the filling, put the spinach in a large pan of water, cover and cook gently, stirring occasionally, for 5–6 minutes until wilted. Drain thoroughly in a colander. Wipe the pan dry, add the olive oil and sauté the onion and spring onions until translucent. Add the spinach and salt and pepper, and sauté for 4–5 minutes. Let cool.

Beat the eggs in a large bowl, crumble in the feta, add the herbs, milk and spinach, and mix well with a fork.

Unroll the pastry carefully – you will have an oblong stack of paper-thin sheets. Brush the roasting pan with the melted butter, then butter sparingly the top sheet of pastry and lay it into the pan, folding any excess on one side (keep in mind that the pastry will shrink when cooked). Continue the same way, folding the excess on alternate ends until you have used about half the pastry.

Add the filling and spread it evenly. Fold the sides over it and start covering with the remaining pastry sheets, brushing each one with melted butter. Finally, brush the top layer of pastry generously with butter. Using a sharp knife, score the top layers of pastry into diamonds or squares – do it carefully to avoid spilling the filling.

Using your fingertips, sprinkle a little cold water on top to stop the pastry curling.

Bake in the preheated oven for 50 minutes until golden on top. (It is nice to have it still a little moist in the centre.)

Slice carefully and serve hot or at room temperature.

SPICY MEAT PASTRIES

Also known as *sambusak*, these are intricate little pastries with sweet and sour flavours and delicious aromas.

175 g/1⅓ cups plain/all-purpose flour, plus extra for dusting

½ tsp salt

2 tbsp olive oil

1 egg yolk, lightly beaten

FILLING

3–4 tbsp olive oil

1 large onion, finely chopped

200 g/7 oz. lean minced/ground lamb

1 tsp ground allspice

1 tsp ground cumin

a large pinch of ground cinnamon

freshly squeezed juice of 1 lemon

3 tbsp raisins, rinsed

150 ml/⅔ cup hot water

3 tbsp finely chopped mint

2 tbsp pine nuts, toasted in a dry frying pan/skillet

salt and black pepper

round 8-cm/3-inch pastry cutter

baking sheet, oiled

MAKES ABOUT 30

To make the pastry, sift the flour and salt into a bowl. Make a well in the centre, add the oil and mix with your fingers. Add 90 ml/6 tablespoons water and knead until a soft, neat ball is formed. Cover with clingfilm/plastic wrap and let rest for 30 minutes.

For the filling, heat the oil in a saucepan, add the onion and sauté until it turns light brown, about 10 minutes.

Increase the heat and add the minced lamb, turning and breaking up the lumps until all the moisture has evaporated and it starts to sizzle. Add the allspice, cumin, cinnamon, salt and pepper, and brown for 2–3 minutes. Add the lemon juice, raisins and the hot water, then cover and cook for 20 minutes until fairly dry.

Add the mint and pine nuts, then set aside.

Preheat the oven to 200°C (400°F) Gas 6.

Divide the pastry in half. Roll out one piece on a lightly floured surface to a circle about 30 cm/12 inches in diameter.

Cut out rounds with the pastry cutter. Gather the offcuts and add to the remaining portion of pastry. Knead until soft again, then cover and set aside.

Have a small bowl of cold water by you. Put 1 teaspoon of filling in the middle of a round of pastry. Dip a finger in the water and wet the edges, then fold half of the pastry over, making a half-moon shape. Press the edges firmly to seal and put it on the baking sheet. Repeat until all the rounds have been used.

Roll out the remaining pastry, cut out more rounds and repeat the process.

Brush the tops with the egg yolk and bake in a preheated oven for 10–12 minutes until light golden.

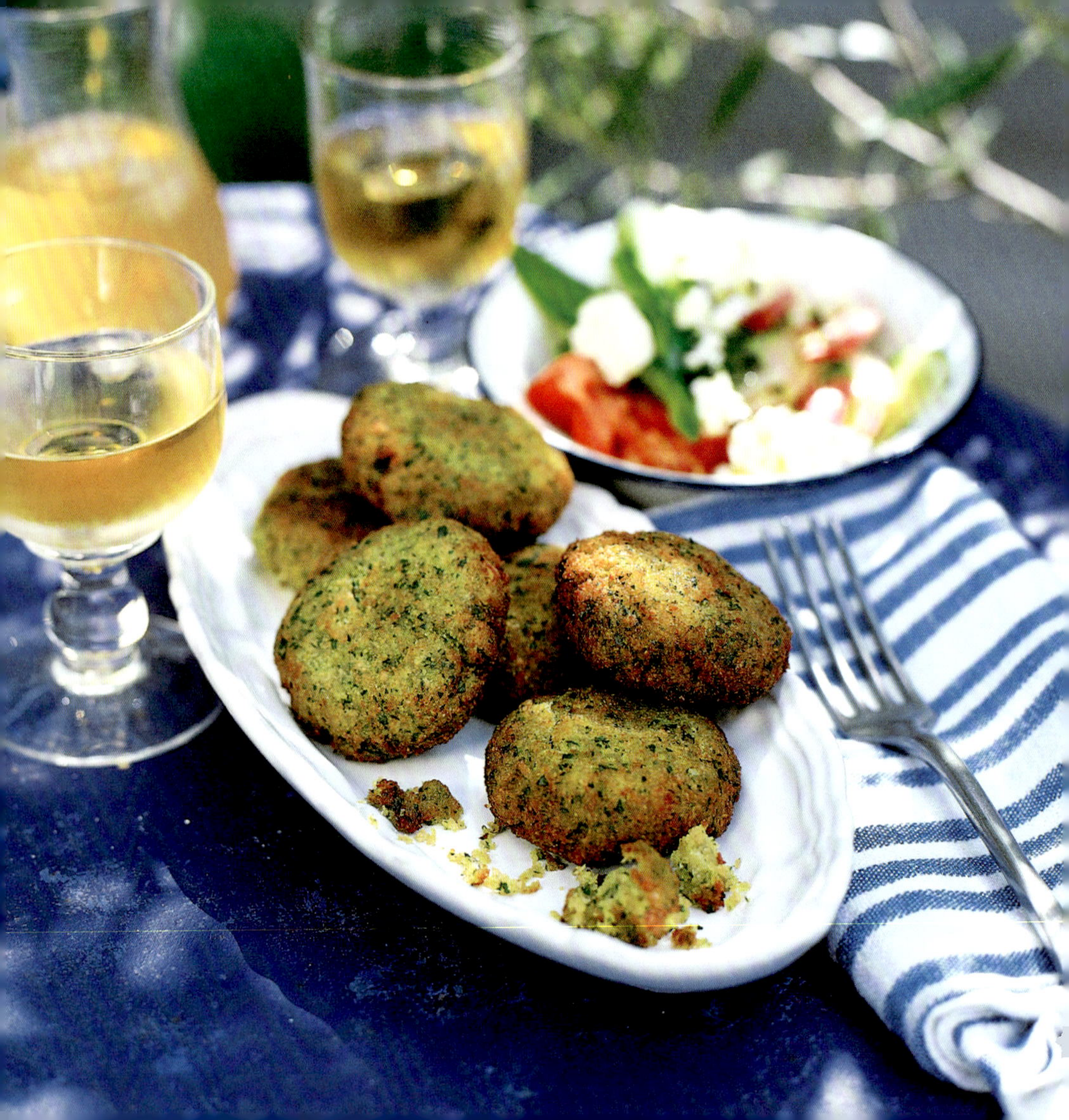

SPICY BROAD BEAN FALAFEL

250 g/9 oz. dried, skinless broad/fava beans, soaked overnight in cold water to cover

1 large onion (about 400 g/ 14 oz.), coarsely chopped

2 garlic cloves, crushed

1 tbsp ground cumin

1 tbsp ground coriander

1 tsp ground allspice

¼ tsp cayenne pepper

¼ tsp baking powder

a bunch of flat-leaf parsley (about 200 g/2½ cups)

a handful of coriander/cilantro

groundnut or sunflower oil, for deep-frying

MAKES ABOUT 20

Falafel are very good served with Roasted Red Pepper and Chickpea Hummus (see page 12), Tarator (see page 16) or Tzatziki (see page 16), and a refreshing salad.

Drain and rinse the soaked beans. Put them in a food processor, then add the onion, garlic, cumin, ground coriander, allspice, cayenne pepper and baking powder. Process to an almost-smooth paste – a little texture is good.

Add the parsley and coriander and process briefly; the greenery should be coarsely chopped and identifiable. (You may have to halve the ingredients and process in two batches, depending on the size of your processor). Empty into a bowl and set aside for at least 1 hour.

Take 1 tablespoon of the mixture and shape it between your palms into a flat round shape, about 5 cm/2 inches in diameter. Continue until all the mixture has been used.

Just before serving, heat 1 cm/½ inch depth of oil in a large non-stick frying pan/skillet, add a single layer of the falafels and fry until golden and crisp on one side. Turn them over to crisp on the other side, then remove with a slotted spoon and drain on a plate lined with paper towels. Repeat until all the falafels have been fried.

They are delicious served hot or at room temperature.

SPICY HARISSA FALAFEL

Freshly made falafel are delicious. These ones are laced with Moroccan harissa paste, which gives a delicious hint of warming spice, complemented here by the cooling Greek yogurt.

2 x 400-g/14-oz. cans chickpeas/garbanzo beans, drained

1 small white onion, chopped

2 garlic cloves, chopped

1 tbsp ground cumin, plus a pinch to garnish

1½ tbsp coriander seeds, lightly crushed

a small bunch of flat-leaf parsley (stalks and leaves)

a small bunch of coriander/cilantro (stalks and leaves), plus a few sprigs to garnish

1 tsp baking powder

1 tsp salt

65 g/½ cup plain/all-purpose flour

30 ml/2 tbsp harissa paste, plus extra to serve

vegetable oil, for deep-frying

TO SERVE
Greek yogurt

nigella seeds

SERVES 4

Place half the chickpeas and all the onion, garlic, cumin, coriander seeds, parsley and coriander, baking powder, salt, flour and harissa paste in a food processor. Blend until just incorporated (be careful not to over-blend to a purée). Once fully incorporated, add the remaining chickpeas and pulse until broken down but still quite coarse (this gives your falafel texture).

Roll the mixture into falafel the size of ping-pong balls, then flatten slightly with the palm of your hand.

Heat the oil in a large saucepan; test whether it is hot enough by dropping a pinch of breadcrumbs into

– they should sizzle immediately but take at least 30 seconds before they turn golden. Deep-fry the falafel in the hot oil for 2–4 minutes until the exterior is crisp (you might need to do this in batches). Remove the cooked falafel using a slotted spoon and leave on paper towels to drain any excess oil.

To serve, pour some Greek yogurt onto a large serving dish and swirl a couple of ribbons of harissa paste through the yogurt to create beautiful swirls. Pile the falafel over one side of the yogurt, then dust with an extra pinch of cumin, a pinch of nigella seeds and a few sprigs of fresh coriander.

PASTRIES, PATTIES & BREADS

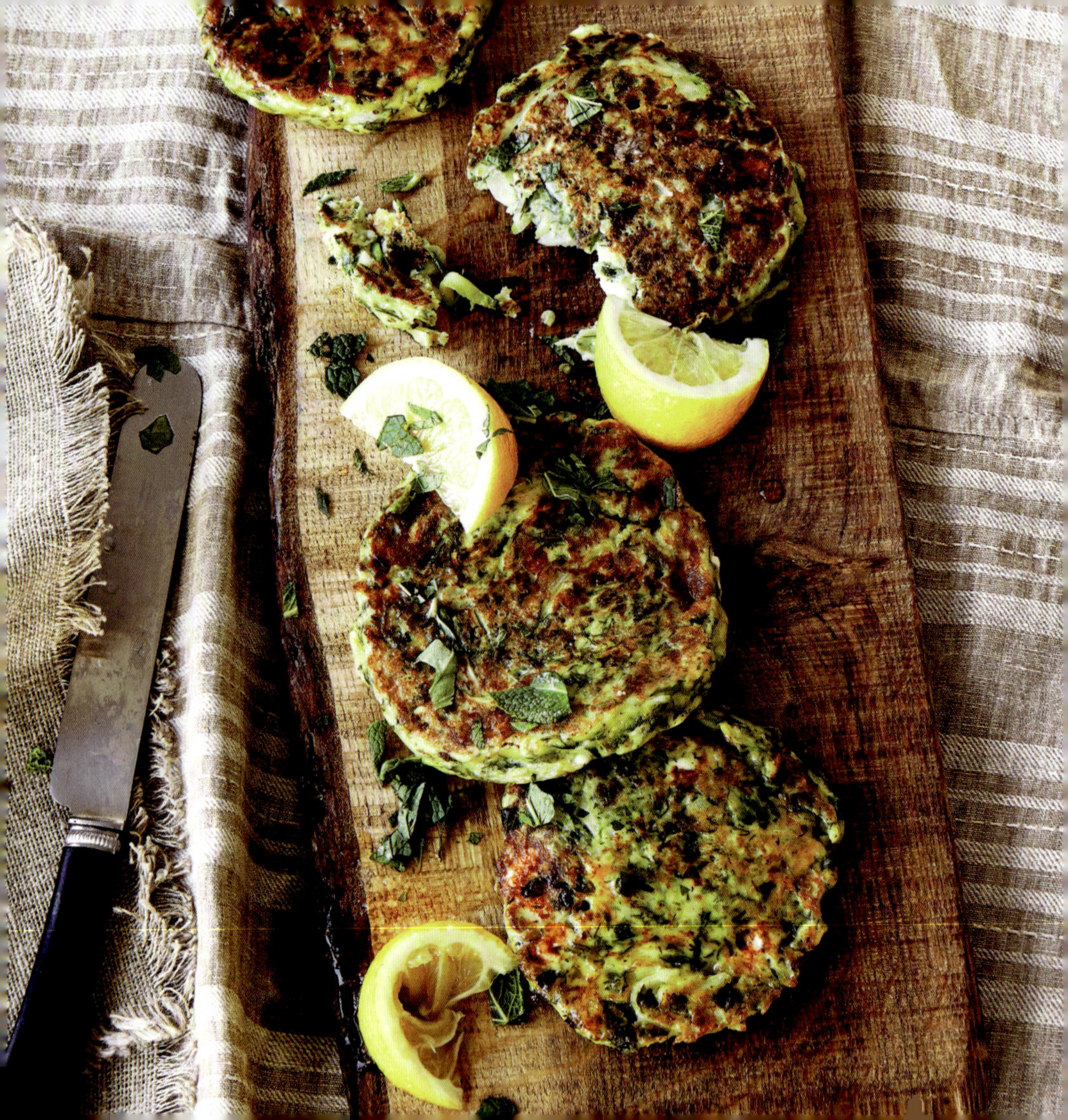

COURGETTE, FETA & HERB PATTIES

3 eggs

3 tbsp plain/all-purpose flour

2 firm courgettes/zucchini

1 red or gold onion, cut in half lengthways, in half again crossways, and sliced with the grain

200 g/7 oz. feta, crumbled

1–2 fresh red or green chillies/chiles, deseeded and finely chopped

2 tsps dried mint

a bunch of flat-leaf parsley, coarsely chopped

a bunch of dill fronds, coarsely chopped

a big bunch of mint, coarsely chopped, plus extra to garnish

sunflower oil, for frying

salt and black pepper

lemon wedges, to serve

SERVES 6

These fried patties should be packed with herbs – the more the merrier. You can also use grated raw carrot or fried leeks in them, if you like.

In a big bowl, beat the eggs with the flour until smooth.

Trim off the ends of the courgettes, but don't peel them. Grate the courgettes on the coarse side of a grater, then squeeze out all the water with your hands. Pile the courgette on top of the flour and egg mixture. Add the onion, feta, chillies, dried mint and fresh herbs, and mix well with a large spoon or your hand. Season well with salt and pepper.

Heat a little sunflower oil in a heavy-based frying pan/skillet – don't put in too much oil; you can always add more as you fry the patties.

Place 2–3 spoonfuls of the courgette mixture into the pan and fry over a medium heat for about 2 minutes each side, pressing the patties down a little with the spatula, so that they are flat but quite thick, lightly browned and firm. Cook the patties in batches, adding more oil to the pan when necessary, then drain on paper towels, and keep the cooked ones warm under aluminium foil, or in a warm oven.

Arrange the patties on a serving dish, garnish with extra mint, and serve with wedges of lemon to squeeze over them.

TOMATO KEFTEDES

These are simply onion and green herbs bound together with pinched tomato flesh and flour, then fried until dark red. Serve with Tzatziki (see page 16) or try serving alongside Fava (see page 19) instead.

400 g/14 oz. ripe cherry tomatoes

½ red onion, very finely chopped

5 g/¼ cup basil, chopped

10 g/½ cup mint, chopped

1 tsp dried oregano

5 g/¼ cup flat-leaf parsley, chopped

100 g/¾ cup self-raising/self-rising flour

250 ml/1 cup olive oil

750 ml/3 cups sunflower oil

salt and black pepper

Tzatziki (see page 16), to serve

MAKES 16

Put the tomatoes in a large bowl and pinch them so that the juices spurt out (be careful to pinch them facing downwards, otherwise you'll end up with pulp in your eye). Keep pinching and tearing at the flesh until you're left with a pile of seeds, juices and pulp.

Add the onion, basil, mint, oregano, parsley and salt and pepper to the pulp. You can use a potato masher at this point to make sure everything is well incorporated.

Add half the flour and stir. Add the second half slowly. You want a thick and sticky paste the texture of a thick batter.

Heat the oils in a deep, heavy-based pan until small bubbles form on the surface. Make sure the oil is at least 5 cm/2 inches deep. Use a greased tablespoon to drop in the batter. After 30 seconds, rotate the fritter so it doesn't stick to the bottom. Fry for another 30 seconds or until the outside is crispy and deep red. Drain well on paper towels. Fry no more than 3 at a time.

Season the fritters with salt and serve hot with tzatziki.

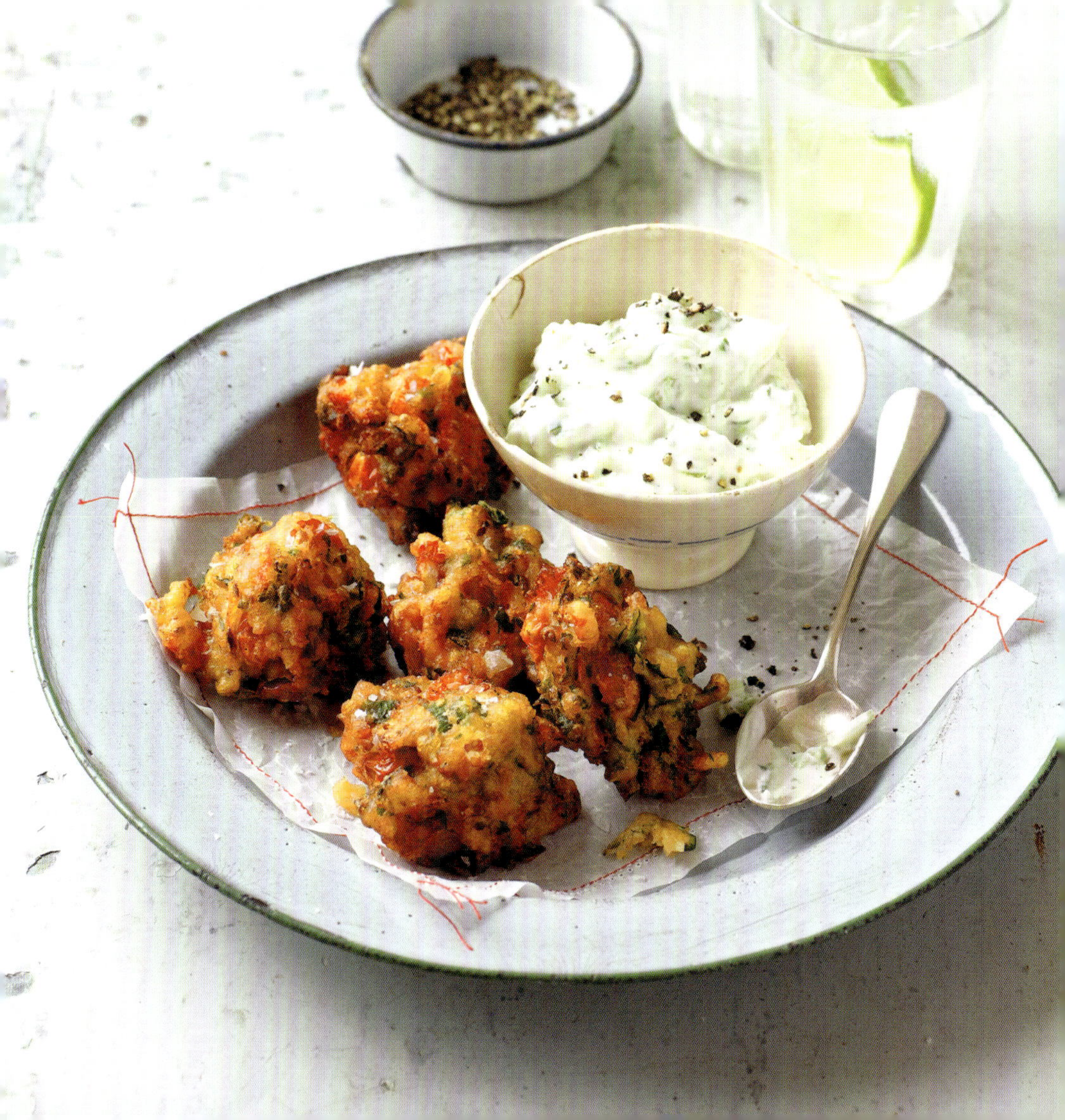

FENNEL SEED & SEA SALT PITTA CHIPS

(see page 5 for image)

These pitta chips are so easy to make but they taste so good! The combination of smoky paprika, zingy fennel seeds and spicy heat make them terribly moreish and ideal for mopping up the delicious dips in your mezze selection.

4 store-bought pitta breads

60 ml/¼ cup olive oil

½ tsp smoked paprika

½ tsp mild or hot chilli/chili powder

1 tsp cumin seeds

½ tbsp sea salt flakes

black pepper

MAKES ABOUT 40

Preheat the oven to 200°C (400°F) Gas 6.

Pittas have a natural pocket so split each pitta to give you two whole sides of pitta and stack them on top of each other. Use a large sharp knife to cut them widthways into 5-cm/2-inch strips.

Put the pitta strips in a large mixing bowl and drizzle over the olive oil. Add all the remaining ingredients and toss until the pitta strips are well coated in oil and seasoning.

Arrange the pitta on a large baking sheet and sprinkle over any leftover spices from the bowl. Bake in the preheated oven for about 12 minutes, or until crisp.

Remove from the oven and leave to cool before arranging them on your mezze board, within easy reach of the delicious dips.

MOROCCAN COUNTRY BREAD

Good bread is essential to scoop or mop up those delicious dips that take centre stage in a mezze selection.

½ tsp fast-action dried yeast

1 tsp sugar

450 g/3½ cups plain/all-purpose flour, plus extra for dusting

75 g/⅔ cup cornmeal/polenta, plus extra for dusting

1 tsp salt

2 tbsp melted butter or ghee

500 ml/2 cups lukewarm water

sesame seeds, for sprinkling

2 baking sheets, oiled

MAKES 2 LOAVES

Put the yeast and sugar in a small bowl with about 60 ml/⅓ cup water. Sift the flour, cornmeal and salt into a large bowl. Make a well in the centre and pour in the dissolved yeast mixture and melted butter. Gradually add the water, using your hands to draw in the flour from the sides to form the mixture into a dough. Add more flour if the dough gets too sticky.

Turn the dough out on to a floured surface and knead until it becomes smooth and elastic. Divide the dough into two pieces. Knead each piece into a ball, then flatten and stretch them into circles, roughly 20 cm/8 inches in diameter.

Dust the oiled baking sheets with cornmeal. Place 1 round of dough on each baking sheet and sprinkle with sesame seeds. Cover them a damp cloth and leave them in a warm place for a bout 1 hour until they doubled in size.

Preheat the oven 220°C(425°F) Gas 7.

Pinch the top of each loaf with your fingers, or prick them with a fork. Pop them into the preheated oven and bake for 15 minutes, then reduce the heat to 180°C (350°F) Gas 4 and bake for a further 15 minutes until the loaves are crusty and golden and sound hollow when tapped on the bottom.

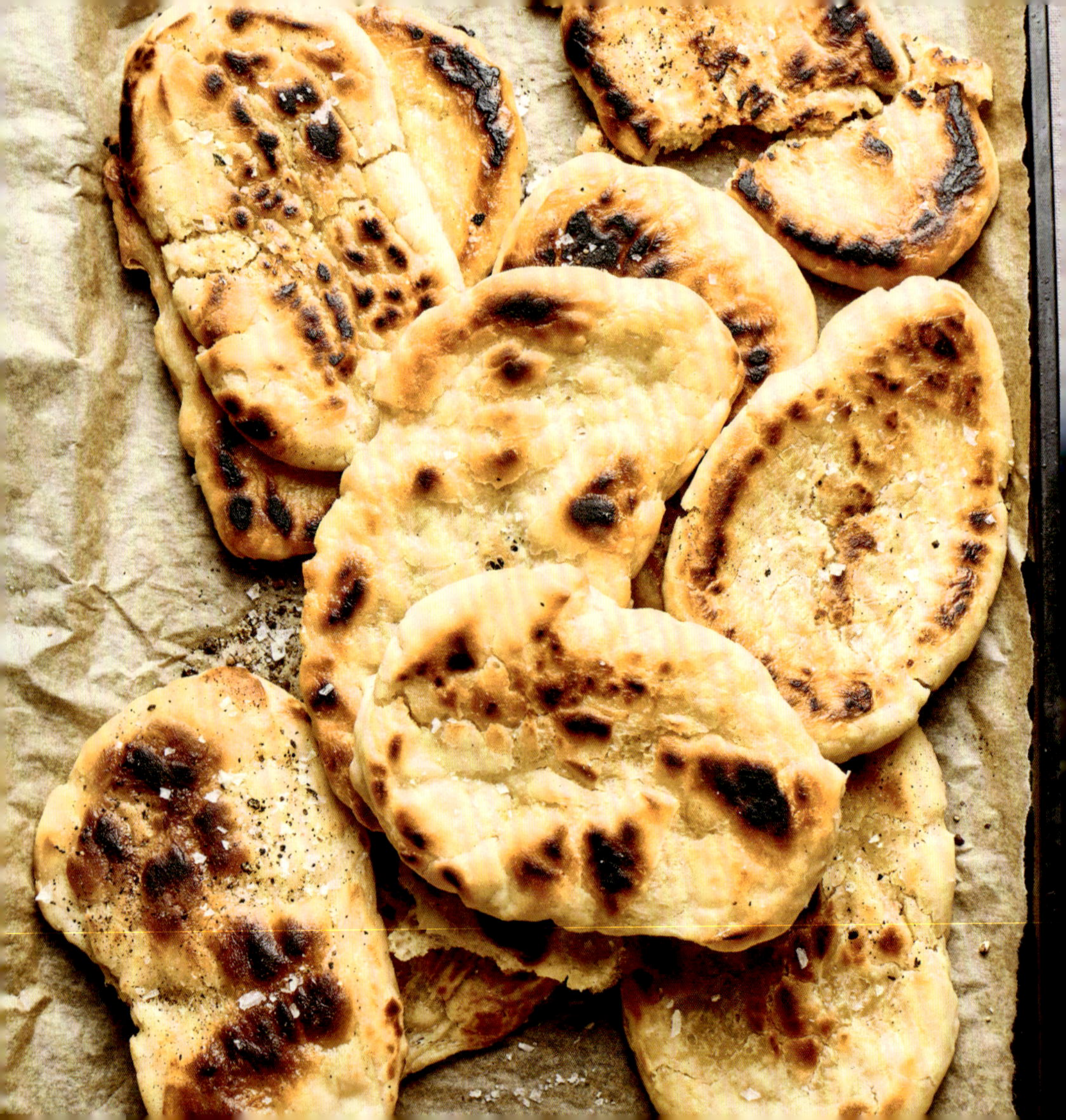

YOGURT PITTA

These super quick and easy yogurt flatbreads are made with a combination of simple ingredients, and are light and fluffy.

7-g/¼-oz. sachet of fast-action dried yeast

200 ml/scant 1 cup warm water

450 g/3¼ cups strong bread flour

1 tsp salt

3 tbsp extra virgin olive oil, plus extra for greasing

200 g/7 oz. Greek yogurt

2 baking sheets, lined

MAKES 8–10 SMALL–MEDIUM PITTAS OR 5–6 LARGE ONES

Mix the yeast in the water (making sure the water is not too hot).

Combine the flour and salt in a stand mixer with the dough hook attachment. Add the yeast mixture, oil and yogurt and mix to combine. Knead the dough, adding more flour if needed, for about 7–10 minutes until it's soft and slightly sticky. Transfer the dough to an oiled bowl, cover with a clean tea/dish towel, and leave to rise for about 2 hours until it has doubled in size.

Preheat the oven to 220°C (425°F) Gas 7.

Turn the dough out onto a clean work surface and divide it into equal balls (the number depends on the size of pittas you are making). Cover and leave to rise for another 20 minutes.

Roll the dough balls out into circles that are 1 cm/½ inch thick. Place a few on the lined baking sheet with space between them.

Bake in batches until they're puffy and lightly browned on top. Begin checking after 5 minutes, rotating the baking sheet if one side of the pittas is puffing up more than the other. Cook for another 3 minutes, then transfer the pittas to a wire rack to cool.

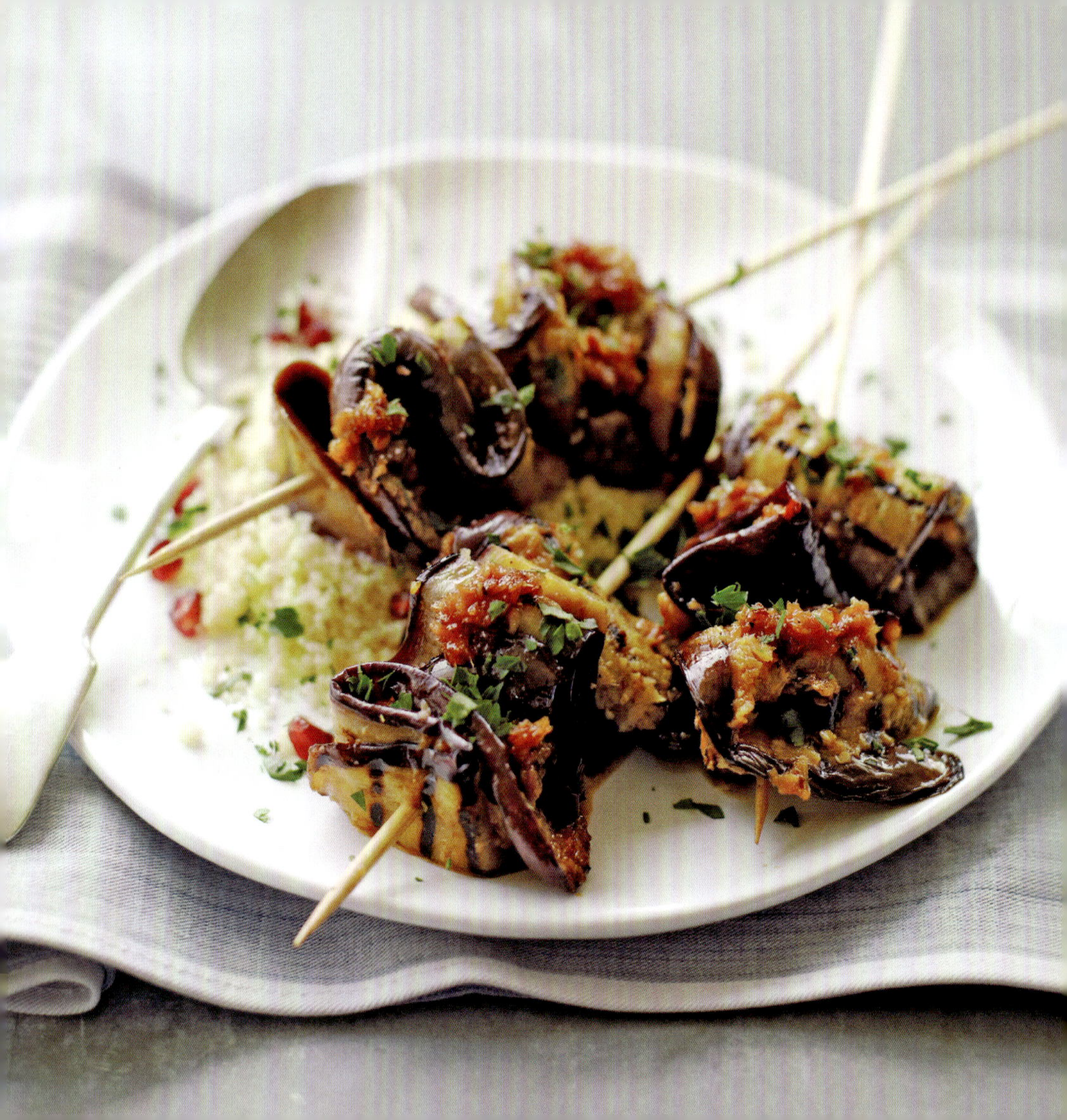

3
SALADS & VEGGIE PLATES

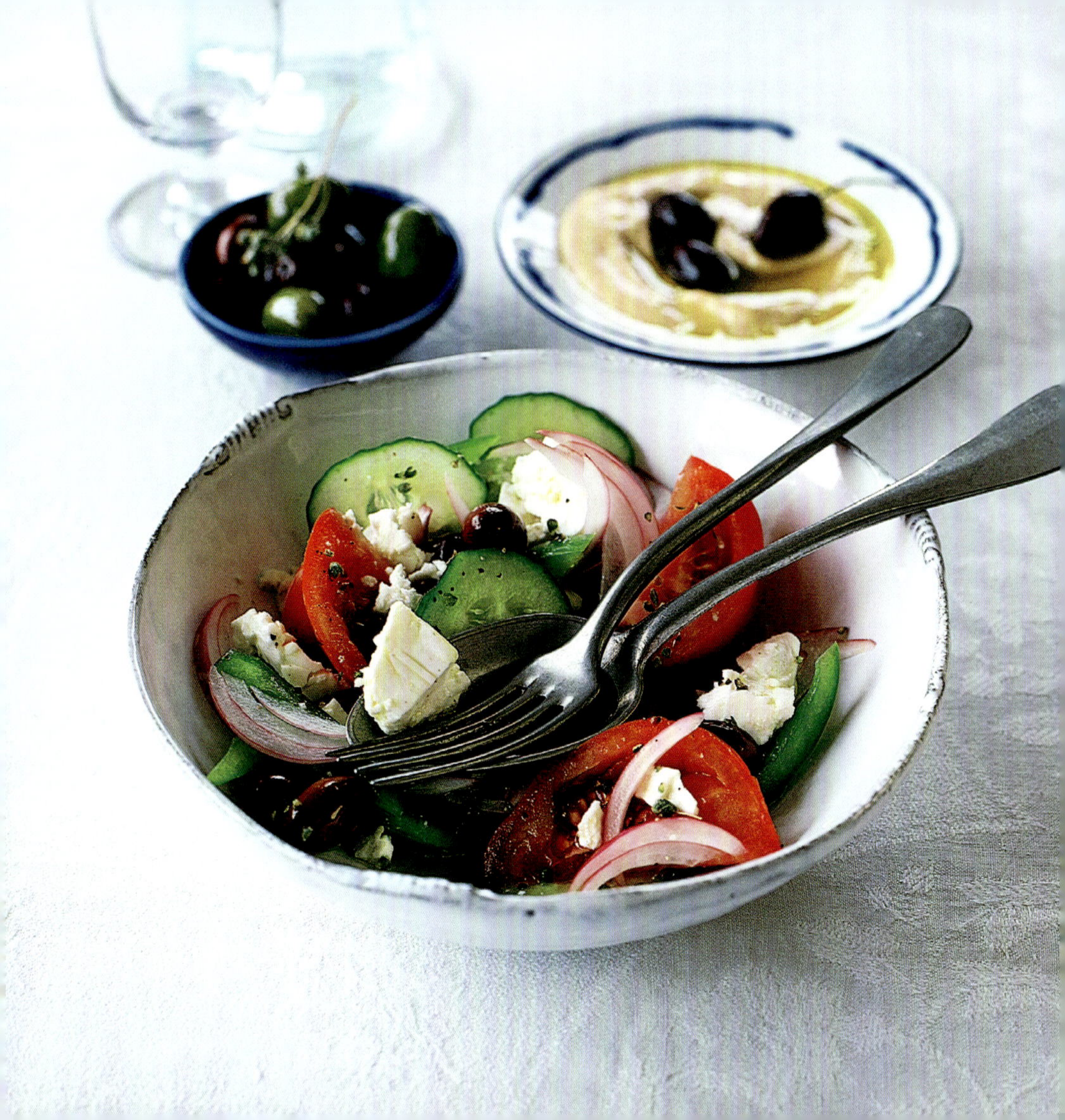

TOMATO, CUCUMBER, ONION & FETA SALAD

400 g/14 oz. ripe sweet tomatoes

1 small red onion, thinly sliced

1 green (bell) pepper, deseeded and sliced into thin ribbons

10-cm/4-inch piece of cucumber, thinly sliced

150 g/5 oz. feta cheese, crumbled

6–8 stoned/pitted black or green olives

5–6 tbsp extra virgin olive oil

a large pinch of dried oregano

salt and black pepper

SERVES 6

Summers in Greece would not be complete without *horiatiki salata*, which can be a meal in itself, as well as a mezze plate. *Horiatiki* means 'peasant or country salad' and it is derived from the word *horio*, meaning 'village'. It is delicious made with ripe sweet tomatoes and a generous amount of an aromatic olive oil. It is even better eaten under a magnificent olive tree beside a dazzling beach and makes a perfect partner for many mezze dishes, particularly grilled kebabs/kabobs and fried vegetables or cheese pies.

Cut the tomatoes in quarters lengthways and cut out the stalk pieces. Cut the quarters into bite-sized wedges and put in a bowl. Add the onion, green (bell) pepper, cucumber, feta cheese, olives, olive oil, oregano, salt and pepper, and toss to coat with the olive oil and infuse with the oregano.

Keep at room temperature for at least 30 minutes to allow the flavours to develop before serving.

TABBOULEH

85 g/½ cup coarse bulgur wheat

a bunch of flat-leaf parsley (about 200 g/2½ cups), trimmed of thick stalks, leaves and stems coarsely chopped

a small bunch of mint, leaves chopped

10-cm/4-inch piece of cucumber, peeled and finely chopped

1 red onion or 4 spring onions/scallions, finely chopped

2 tomatoes (about 250 g/9 oz.), peeled and diced

½ green (bell) pepper, deseeded and finely chopped

lettuce leaves or vine leaves, to serve

VINAIGRETTE

freshly squeezed juice of 1–2 lemons

4–5 tbsp extra virgin olive oil

a large pinch of ground allspice

salt and black pepper

SERVES 6

Tabbouleh is the crown of Lebanese mezze. It is predominantly a green herby salad full of aromas, so the proportion of wheat to herbs is vital. Ideally herbs should always be chopped by hand rather than mashed up in a food processor.

Put the bulgur in a fine sieve/strainer and rinse it under cold running water. Put in a bowl and soak in warm water for 20 minutes. Drain and pat dry in a clean tea/dish towel to get rid of excess moisture. Transfer to a large bowl.

Add the parsley, mint, cucumber, onion, tomatoes and pepper, then mix well. Cover with clingfilm/plastic wrap and chill lightly.

Just before serving, make the vinaigrette. Put the juice of 1 lemon in a bowl, add the olive oil, allspice, salt and pepper and beat lightly. Pour over the salad and toss.

Adjust the seasoning to taste, adding more lemon juice, if needed for a refreshing tangy taste. Line a bowl with lettuce or vine leaves and heap the salad on top.

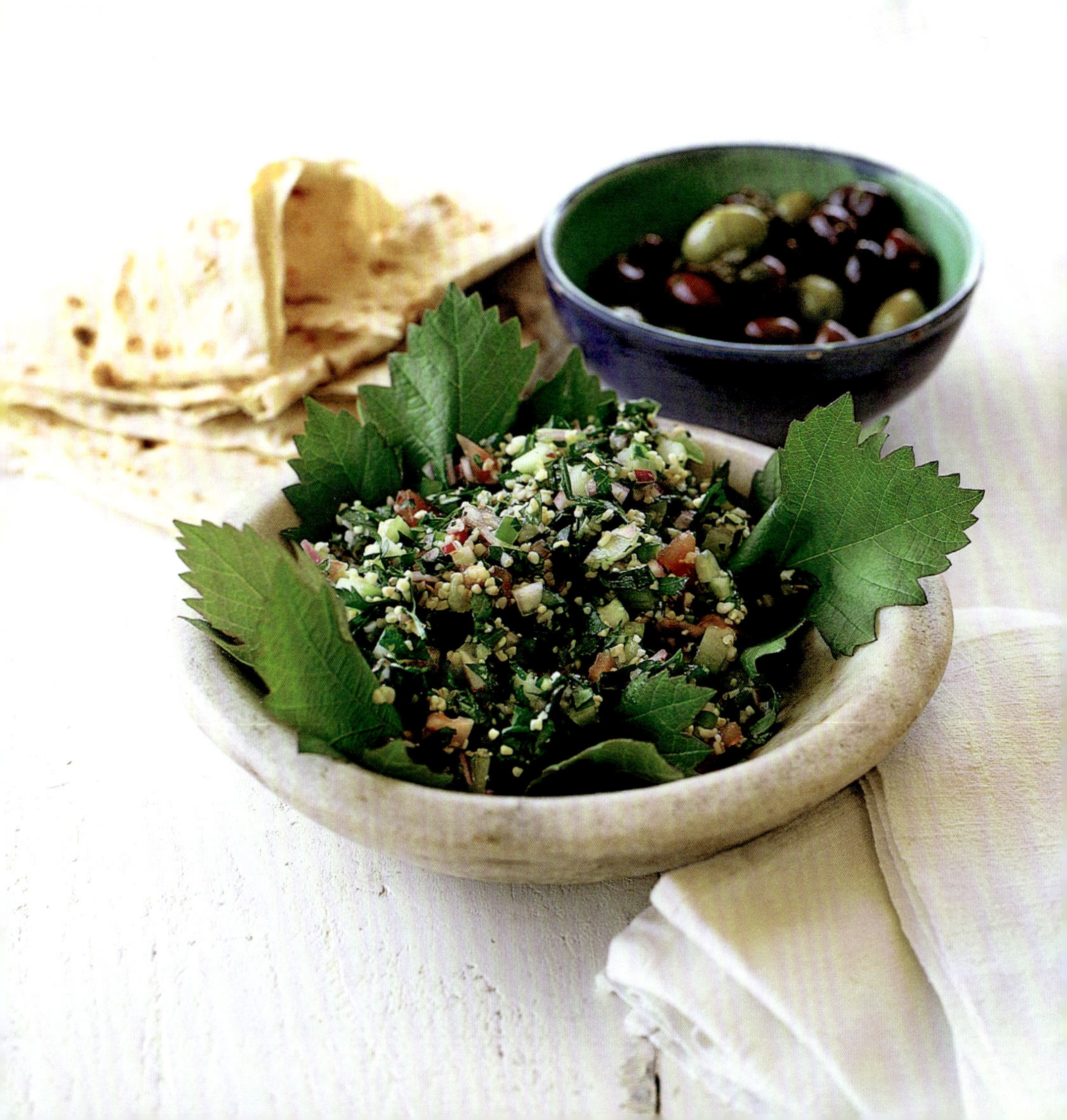

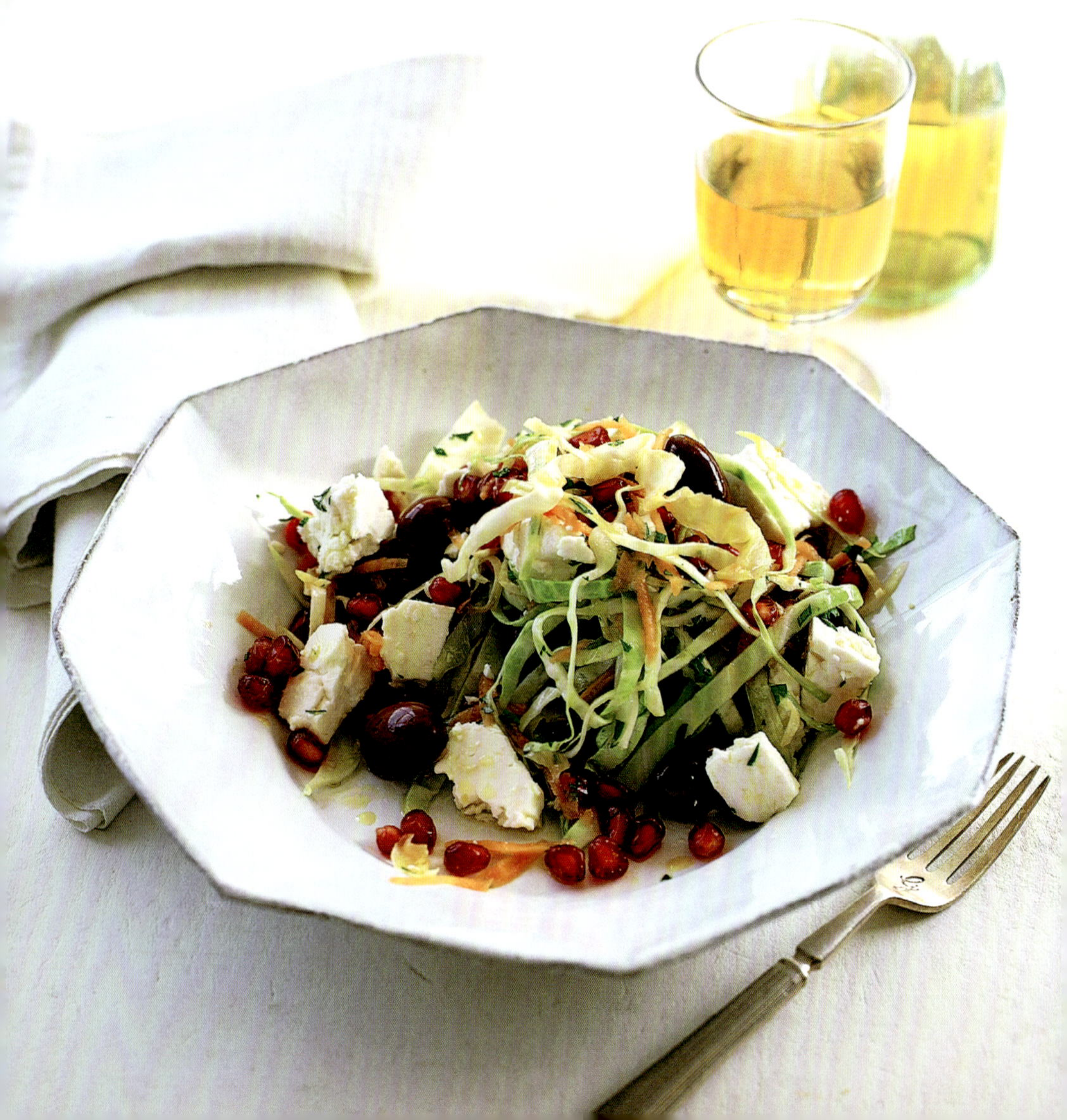

CABBAGE SALAD WITH POMEGRANATE

1 white cabbage

1 pomegranate

2 carrots, scraped and grated

2–3 tbsp finely chopped flat-leaf parsley

100 g/3½ oz. feta, cut into cubes

6–8 stoned/pitted green or black olives

VINAIGRETTE

6 tbsp extra virgin olive oil

freshly squeezed juice of 1 lemon

1 garlic clove, crushed

salt

SERVES 6

This is the winter salad *par excellence* in Greece when you find its refreshing taste everywhere on the Greek table. Greek cooks pride themselves on how thinly they slice the cabbage. The cheese and pomegranate seeds make this classic salad even harder to resist.

Remove and discard the outer leaves and the hard stem of the cabbage. Cut the head into quarters and trim off any obvious hard bits. Put each quarter on its side and cut long, very thin slices until you reach the central core, which should be discarded.

Cut the pomegranate in quarters, then patiently extract the jewel-like scarlet seeds by hand over a plate to catch all of the delicious juices.

Put the cabbage in a bowl with the carrots, parsley, feta, olives, pomegranate seeds and juices and toss well.

To make the vinaigrette, put the olive oil, lemon juice, garlic and salt in a bowl, and beat well. Pour over the salad, toss until everything is thoroughly coated, then serve.

POMEGRANATE SALAD WITH BASIL

Variations of this refreshing, crunchy salad appear from Iran to Morocco.

1 white onion	a small bunch of basil leaves, shredded
1 tsp salt	
6 pomegranates	**SERVES 4–6**
3–4 tbsp pomegranate syrup/molasses	

Slice the onion in half lengthways, then slice the two halves in half again crossways. Finely slice the quarters. Scatter the strips of onion on a plate, sprinkle with the salt and set aside.

Cut the pomegranate in quarters, then patiently extract the jewel-like scarlet seeds by hand.

Tip the onions into a colander and rinse off all the salt. Drain them on several layers of thick paper towels and pat dry.

Add the onions to the pomegranate seeds and toss in the pomegranate syrup. Toss a few basil leaves through the salad, and garnish with the rest.

CELERY & COCONUT SALAD WITH LIME

Crunchy and creamy with a citrus burst from the fresh lime, this salad is delightfully refreshing on a hot day. It is best prepared with the juicy flesh of a fresh coconut.

6 long celery stalks/sticks, grated (reserve the leaves for the garnish)	3–4 tbsp thick, creamy yogurt
	2 garlic cloves, crushed
½ fresh coconut, grated	salt and black pepper
grated zest and freshly squeezed juice of 1 lime	a few mint leaves, shredded
	SERVES 4

Tip the grated celery and coconut into a bowl. Toss in the lime zest and juice.

Mix the yogurt and garlic and season well with salt and pepper. Tip the mixture onto the celery and coconut and mix well. Leave the salad to sit for 10–15 minutes so that the celery begins to weep a little into the yogurt.

Spoon the salad into a serving bowl, or the empty coconut shells, and garnish with the celery and mint leaves.

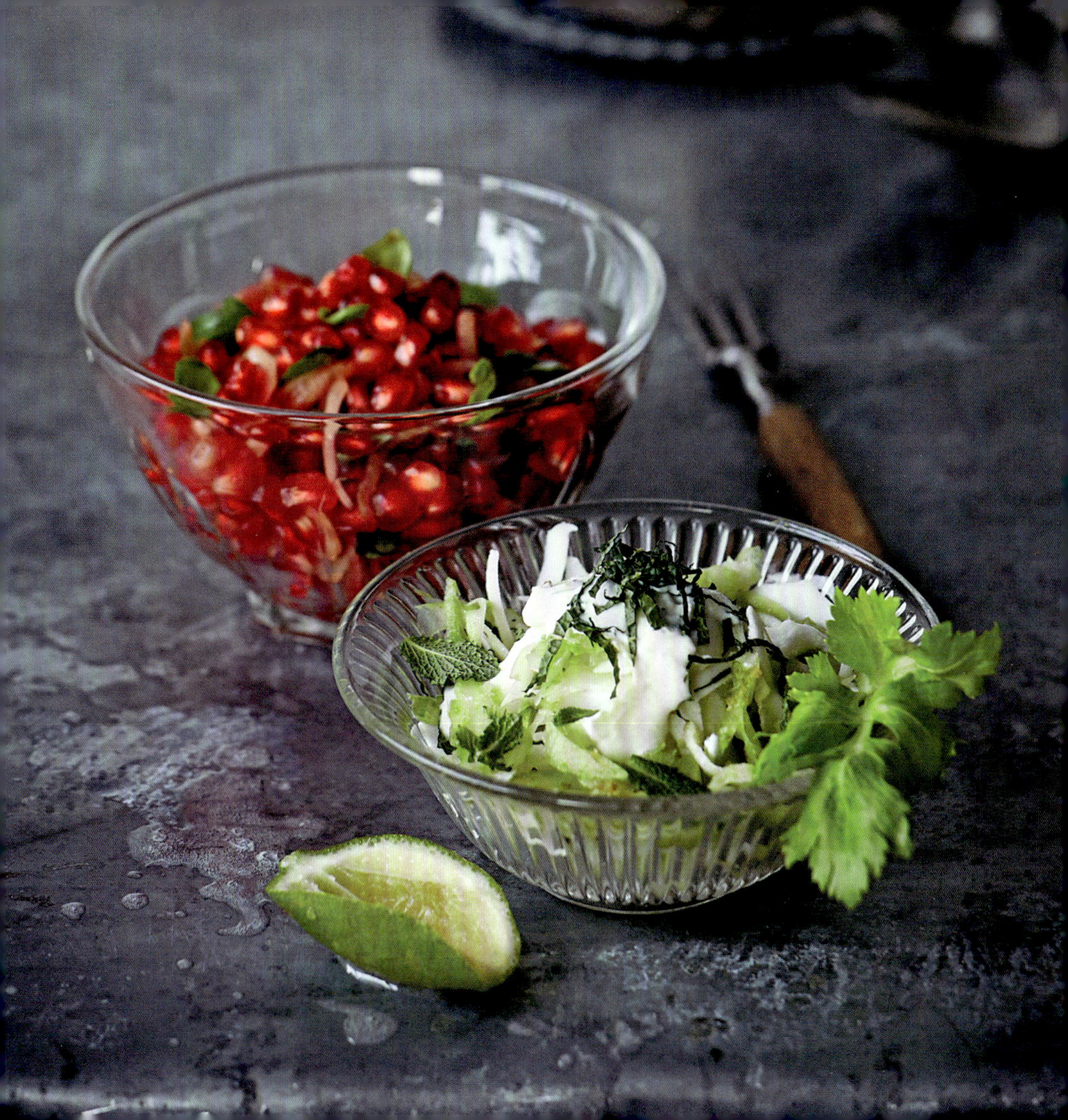

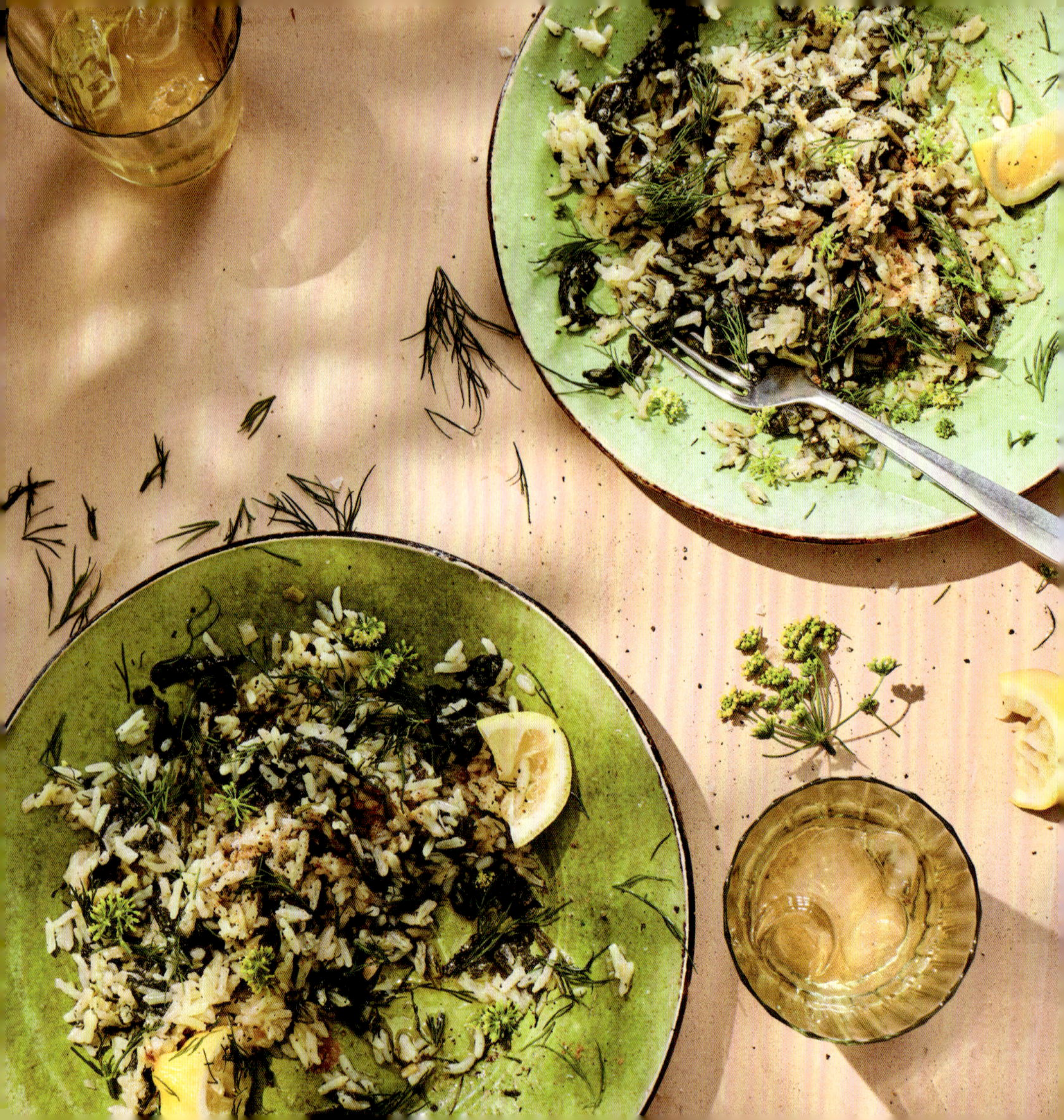

GREEK-STYLE RICE WITH SPINACH, LEEK, DILL & LEMON

Rustic, comforting and a mid-week staple in every Greek home. Simply serve with a chunk of feta and some olives. This dish can be made with a few variations – either just spinach or just leek, or add some chopped tomatoes into it. Spinach, leek and dill is a combination that is both simple and delicious.

100 ml/scant ½ cup extra virgin olive oil

1 onion , finely chopped

2 leeks, thinly sliced

500 g/1 lb. 2 oz. baby spinach leaves, washed and finely chopped

a bunch of dill, finely chopped

300 g/1⅔ cups long-grain rice

freshly squeezed juice of 1–2 lemons

SERVES 4

Heat the oil in a large saucepan over a medium heat. Add the onion and leeks, and gently cook for 10 minutes until softened but not coloured.

Add the spinach and half the dill, and cook over a high heat, stirring regularly, until the spinach has wilted down and all the liquid has evaporated.

Stir in the rice, add 600 ml/2½ cups water and bring to the boil. Turn the heat right down again to a very gentle simmer, cover the pan with a tight-fitting lid and cook for 25–30 minutes, or until the rice has cooked and absorbed all the water. Give it a stir after 15 minutes to ensure even cooking, adding a drop more water as required.

When the rice is cooked, stir in the remaining dill, season well, squeeze over the lemon juice to taste and serve.

BITE-SIZED VEGETABLE ROLLS WITH HALLOUMI

60 g/2 oz. white cabbage, shredded

60 g/2 oz. raw beetroot/beet, peeled and grated

a handful of coriander/cilantro, coarsely chopped

a handful of mint leaves, coarsely chopped

1 tbsp freshly squeezed lemon juice

2 aubergines/eggplants

200 g/7 oz. halloumi

4 tbsp hummus

4 tbsp toasted almonds, coarsely crushed

2 tbsp pomegranate seeds

salt and black pepper

TO FINISH
olive oil
runny honey
pomegranate molasses

MAKES ABOUT 16

These flavoursome charred aubergine/eggplant rolls will keep people coming back for more.

Combine the shredded cabbage, grated beetroot and chopped herbs in a bowl and add a squeeze of lemon juice, a pinch each of salt and pepper and a small drizzle of olive oil.

Slice the aubergines lengthways as thinly as you can get them (about 3 mm/⅛ inch is ideal) and aim for 16 slices. Heat a non-stick griddle/grill pan until hot and cook the strips for about 2 minutes on each side. Repeat until all 16 are done. Set aside.

Keeping the griddle pan hot, cut the halloumi widthways into 1.5-cm/½-inch thick slices and then in half again lengthways to create batons. Place these in the griddle pan and cook for 2 minutes on each side, or until nicely charred. (If you haven't got a non-stick pan, brush the halloumi with a little olive oil).

To assemble the rolls, lay the aubergine slices out flat and spread a teaspoon of hummus over each one. Place a halloumi baton at one end and a heaped tablespoon of the cabbage mixture on top. Add a few drops of honey and a pinch of almonds and pomegranate seeds. Roll the aubergine sup.

Arrange them on a platter, seam-side down, and drizzle with pomegranate molasses and more honey, if liked. Scatter any pomegranate seeds, almonds and herbs still lurking on your chopping board over the top, and serve.

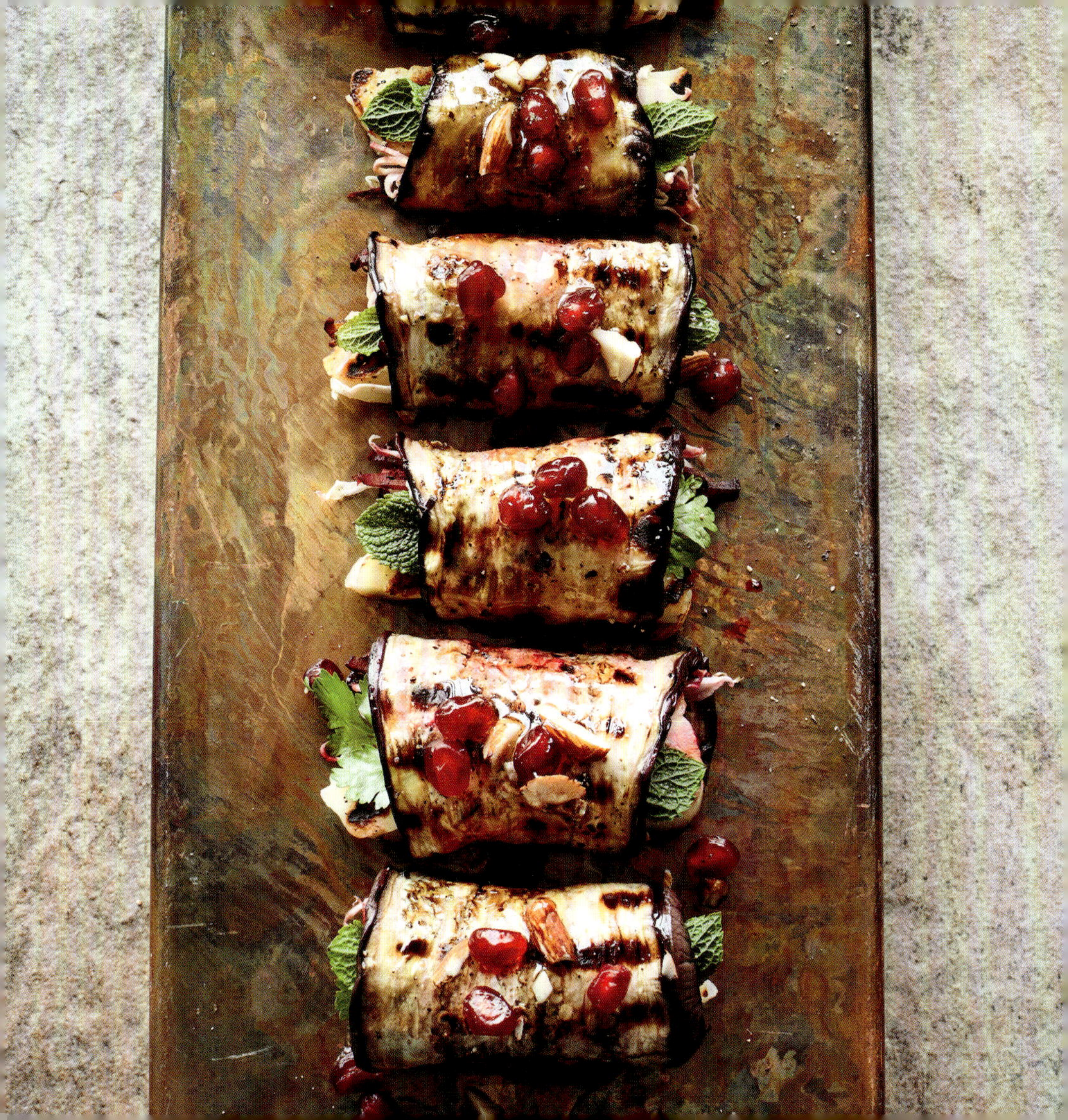

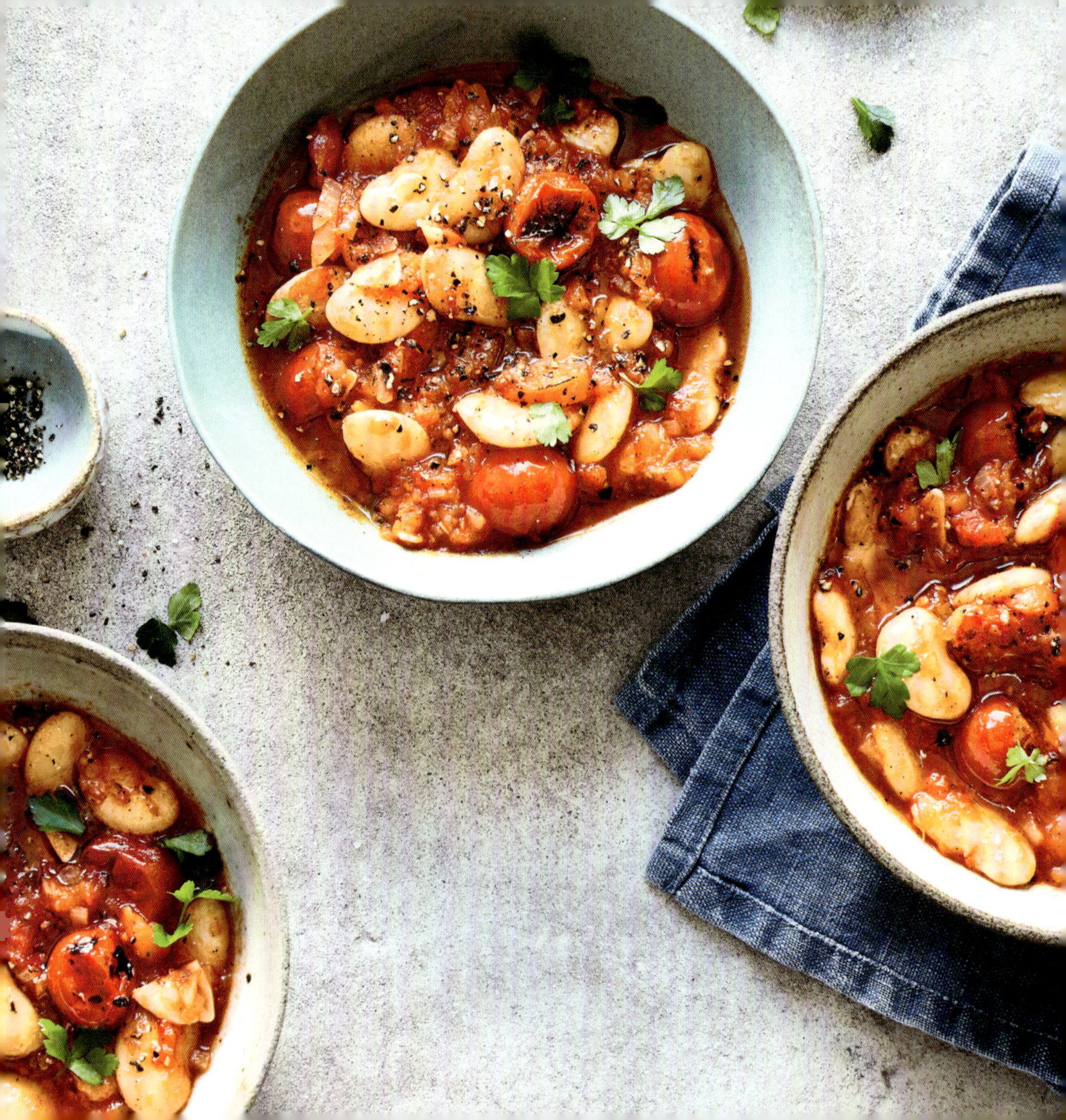

GREEK GIGANTES PLAKI

1 onion, finely chopped

2 garlic cloves, sliced

½ tsp ground cinnamon

½ tbsp coriander seeds, crushed

1 tsp paprika

300-g/10½-oz. can sliced carrots, drained

1 tbsp tomato purée/paste

400-g/14-oz. can cherry tomatoes

400-g/14-oz. can butter beans, drained

½ tsp sugar

salt and black pepper

olive oil, for drizzling

chopped flat-leaf parsley, to serve

SERVES 4

These giant baked beans in tomato sauce are popular throughout the Aegean. This recipe uses canned beans, so these will be good to go within the hour!

Preheat the oven to 180°C (350°F) Gas 4.

In a heavy-based, ovenproof frying pan/skillet, fry the onion in a drizzle of olive oil for 5 minutes until softened, then add the garlic and cook for another minute.

Stir in the cinnamon, crushed coriander seeds and paprika, followed by the carrots, and then mash with a potato masher – this is quite easy and quick. Add a splash more oil if needed, but keep on the heat, and add the tomato purée, can of cherry tomatoes (including all the juices) and the drained butter beans. Fill the cherry tomato can halfway with water, swirl and pour that into the pan (this will be about 250 ml/1 cup water). Finally, season generously with salt, pepper and the sugar and place the whole pan into the preheated oven for 25 minutes.

Once done, remove the pan from the oven and leave to cool for a few minutes before serving. If it's too thick, add a little water to loosen.

Serve hot or at room temperature, with a drizzle of olive oil and chopped parsley scattered over the top.

ROASTED BEETROOT & CARROTS WITH WALNUT SKORDALIA

2–3 raw beetroot/beets (about 500 g/1 lb. 2 oz.), scrubbed and cut into wedges

5 mixed purple and orange carrots (about 500 g/1 lb. 2 oz.), scrubbed and cut in thirds

2 tbsp olive oil

6 sprigs of oregano or 1 tsp dried oregano

salt and black pepper

SKORDALIA

1 potato, peeled and cut into cubes

3 garlic cloves

100 g/¾ cup walnuts, lightly toasted, plus extra to garnish

½ tbsp red wine vinegar

2 tbsp olive oil

salt and black pepper

SERVES 4–6

This is a versatile dish that works brilliantly as part of any mezze spread.

Preheat the oven to 180°C (350°F) Gas 4.

To make the skordalia, place the potato in a small saucepan of water, bring to the boil and cook until very soft. Drain, reserving some of the cooking water.

Using a mortar and pestle crush the garlic with the walnuts until fully combined and become a creamy consistency. Add the garlic and walnut mixture and the vinegar to the potatoes. When they are thoroughly combined, add the oil and mix by hand until you achieve the desired taste. Season with salt and pepper. Place in the fridge for at least 1 hour before you serve. You might find you need a little more vinegar or olive oil to the balance of flavours right.

Place the beetroot, carrots, olive oil, oregano, salt and pepper on a baking sheet and bake for 50–65 minutes until cooked through and crispy on the edges.

Serve on a bed of skordalia, finished with a scattering of extra walnuts.

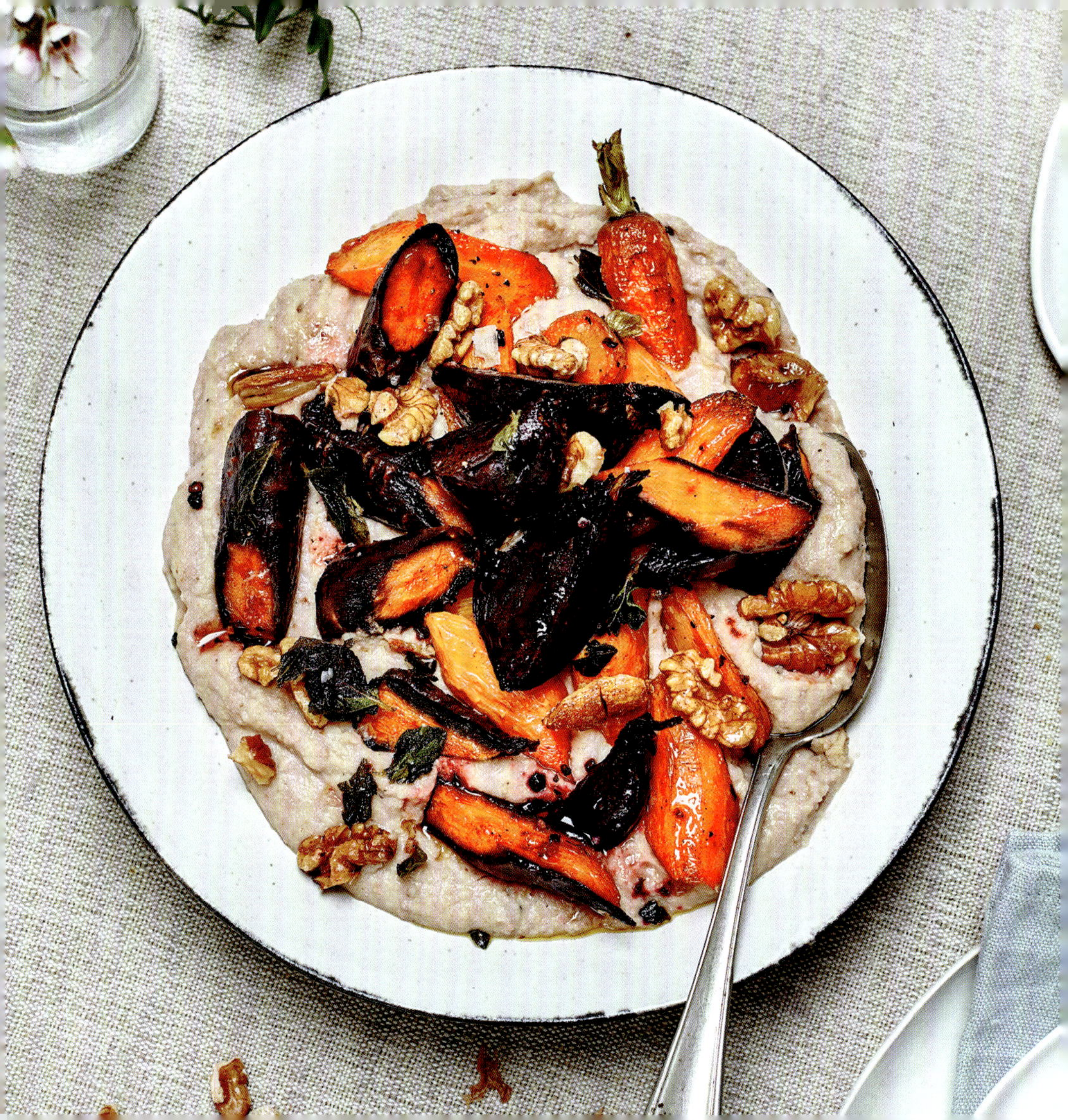

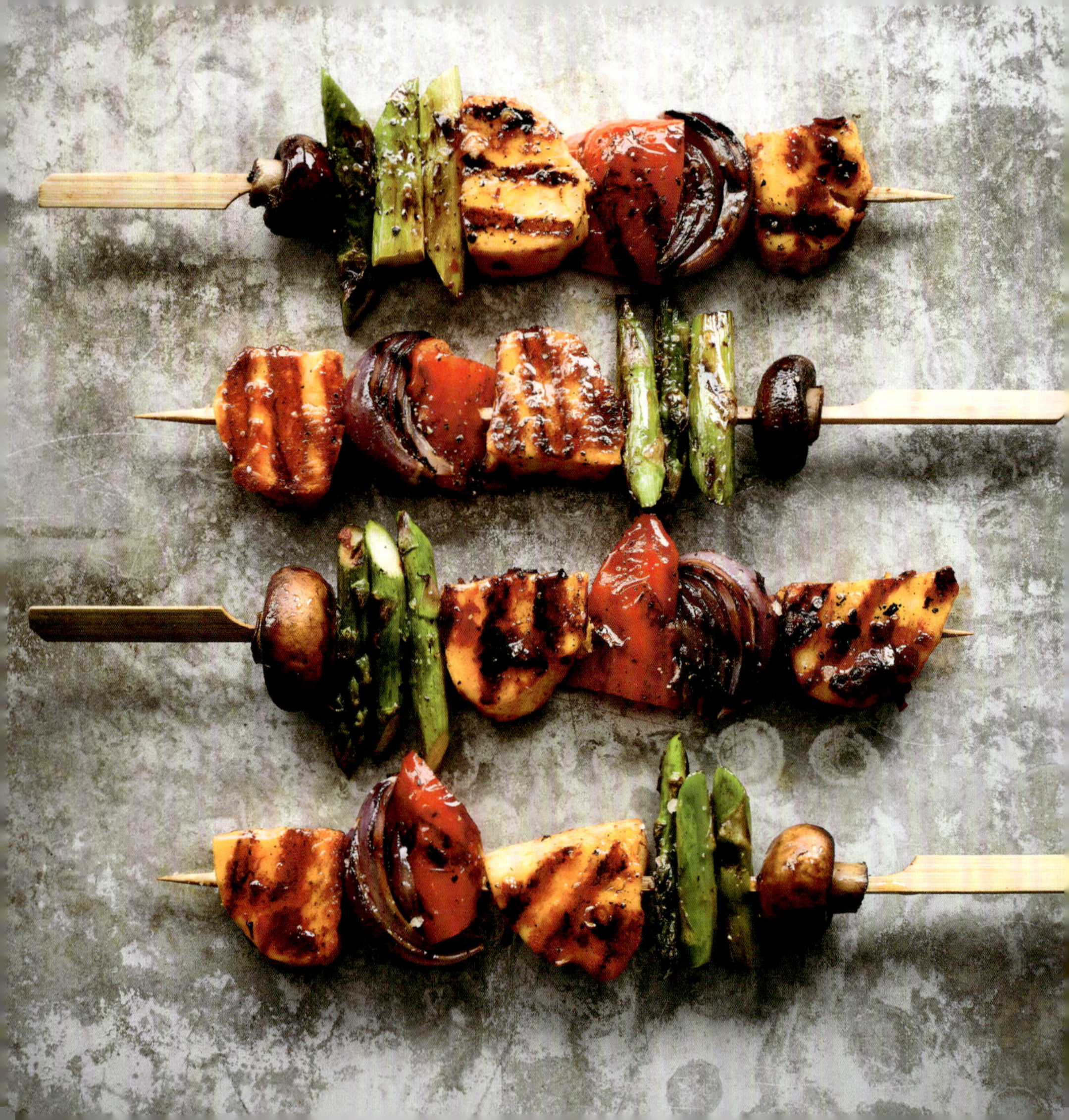

VEGGIE HALLOUMI SOUVLAKI WITH HARISSA

4 tbsp harissa paste

4 tbsp olive oil, plus extra for drizzling

400 g/14 oz. halloumi, cut into bite-sized chunks (12–16 pieces)

1 red (bell) pepper, deseeded and cut into chunks

1 red onion, cut into thick strips

16 button mushrooms

6 asparagus spears, cut into thirds

salt

4 wooden skewers, pre-soaked in water

MAKES 4

The secret to cooking halloumi is, ironically, to treat it like a steak: bring it to room temperature before cooking, sear it at a high heat and stop cooking as soon as the outside has a nice crisp edge. Cooking halloumi over a low heat just dries it out.

Preheat the grill/broiler to really hot.

In a mixing bowl, whisk together the harissa and olive oil. Add the halloumi chunks to the bowl and toss them until coated with the harissa glaze.

Thread the halloumi and vegetables onto the prepared skewers, alternating between different ingredients.

Drizzle over a little olive oil, season with a pinch of salt, and cook under the preheated grill/broiler until the halloumi has started to char, then turn once to cook the other side, removing from the heat as soon as the halloumi is golden.

BAKED AUBERGINES WITH GARLIC & TOMATOES

150 ml/²⁄₃ cup extra virgin olive oil

3 aubergines/eggplants, rinsed and halved lengthways

2 onions, finely chopped

4 garlic cloves, finely chopped

1 tsp ground cumin

500 g/1 lb. 2 oz. ripe tomatoes, chopped

1 tbsp dried oregano

½ tsp sugar

3 tbsp chopped flat-leaf parsley

1 tbsp tomato purée/paste, diluted with 150 ml/²⁄₃ cup hot water

salt and black pepper

SERVES 6

This is a dish full of summer flavours, and it is perfect for mezze as it tastes even better served at room temperature.

Heat half the olive oil in a large frying pan/skillet, add three pieces of aubergine and shallow-fry, turning them over until light golden on both sides, 10–15 minutes. Remove and rest on paper towels. Repeat with the remaining three pieces.

Arrange the pieces side by side in an ovenproof dish and season with salt and pepper.

For the stuffing, heat the remaining olive oil in a saucepan, add the onions and sauté gently until they start to colour. Add the garlic and cumin, fry for 2–3 minutes, then add the tomatoes, oregano, sugar, 150 ml/²⁄₃ cup water, salt and pepper. Cover and cook for 15 minutes, stirring occasionally.

Meanwhile, preheat the oven to 190°C (375°F) Gas 5.

Stir in the parsley, then divide the stuffing mixture into six equal portions. Pile each portion along the length of an aubergine half. Add the diluted tomato purée to the dish and cook in a preheated oven for 45 minutes, basting the aubergines once during cooking.

Serve hot or at room temperature.

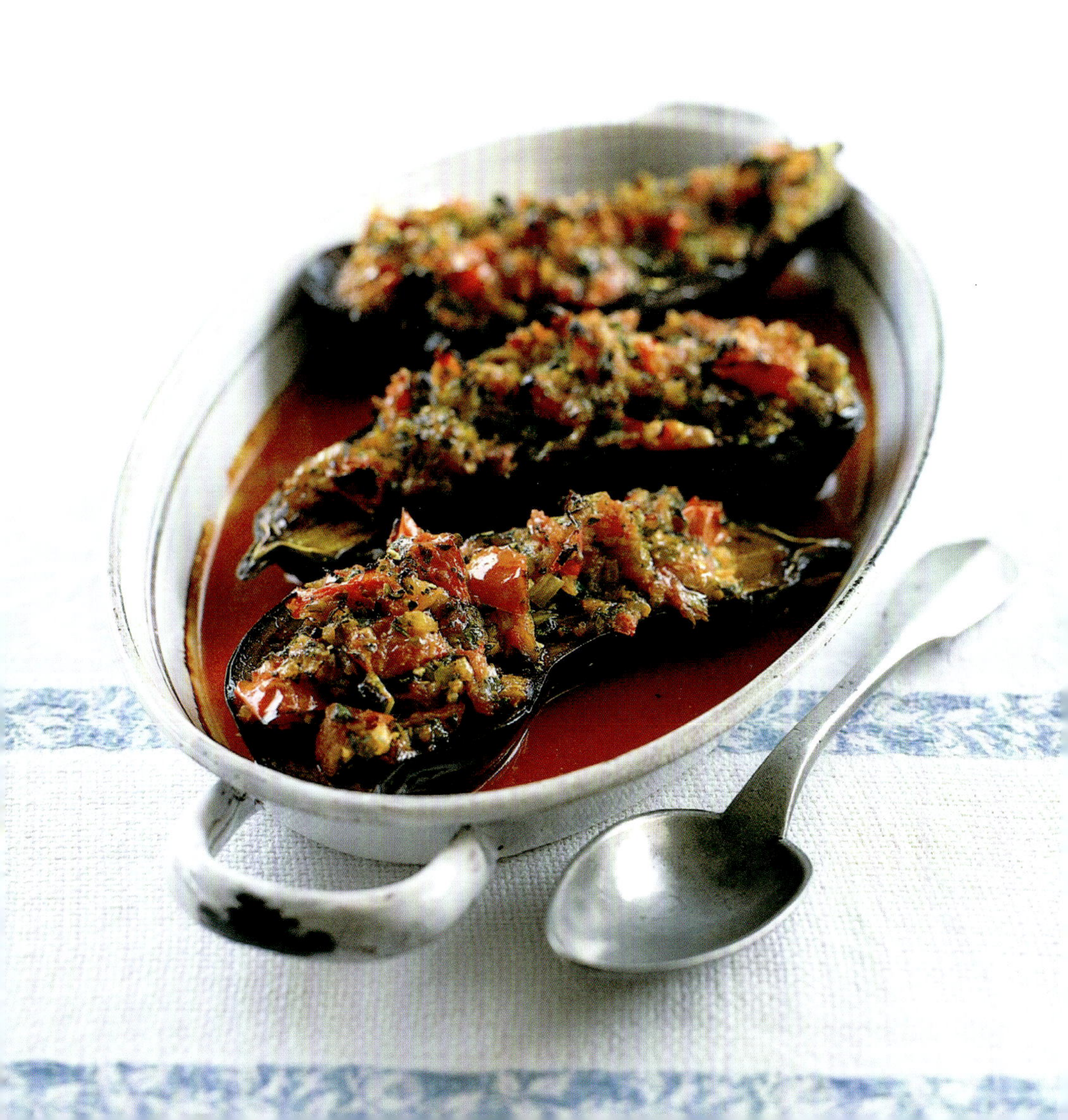

STUFFED VINE LEAVES (DOLMADES)

Dolmades, when made with fresh, young vine leaves in spring, make the most mouthwatering dish in the world for me. There are many versions – they can also be made with a meat stuffing, but this purist's vegetarian version is undoubtedly the star of the show. An exquisite aromatic olive oil is a must. They are time consuming, but invite your friends around for mezze and enlist some help.

55 fresh vine leaves, plus extra to serve, or 225 g/8 oz. preserved vine leaves

4 tbsp extra virgin olive oil

450 ml/2 scant cups hot water

STUFFING

freshly squeezed juice of 1 lemon, strained

150 g/1 cup long-grain rice, rinsed

2 large onions, finely chopped (not grated)

5 spring onions/scallions, trimmed and thinly sliced

4 tbsp finely chopped dill

2 tbsp finely chopped mint

2 tbsp finely chopped flat-leaf parsley

5 tbsp extra virgin olive oil

salt and black pepper

MAKES 50

Bring a large saucepan of water to the boil and blanch the fresh vine leaves for 1–2 minutes in batches of 5–6 at a time. Remove with a slotted spoon and drain in a colander. They should just be wilted. If using preserved leaves, remember they are very salty – rinse first, then soak in a bowl of hot water for 3–5 minutes. Rinse again and drain in a colander.

To make the stuffing, put half the lemon juice in a large bowl. Add all the other ingredients and stir well.

Line the base of a wide saucepan with 4 or 5 vine leaves. Place a vine leaf, rough-side up, on a chopping board (handle the leaves carefully as they are fragile). Put a heaped teaspoon of the stuffing near the stalk end, fold the two opposite sides over the stuffing and roll up tightly like a fat cigar. Repeat with the rest of the leaves.

Arrange the stuffed vine leaves in tight circles in the saucepan with the loose ends underneath. Pour the olive oil and the remaining lemon juice over the top and set a small inverted plate on top to stop them opening up while cooking. Add the hot water, cover and simmer gently for 50 minutes.

Serve hot or at room temperature on a platter lined with fresh vine leaves, if available.

SALADS & VEGGIE PLATES

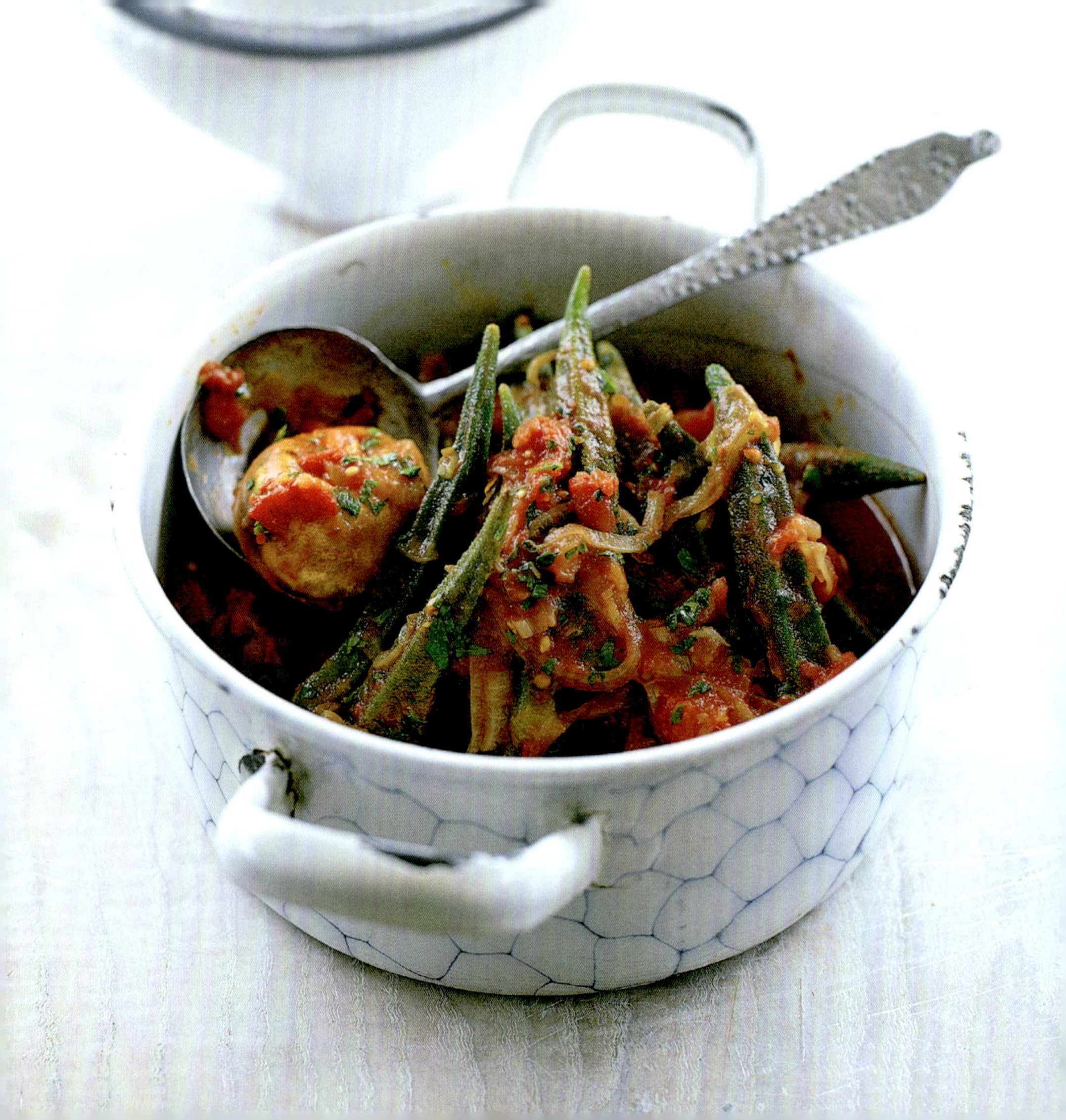

OKRA WITH DRIED LIMES

With its intriguing taste, okra is the beloved vegetable of the Eastern Mediterranean, cooked with or without meat. It is surrounded by an impenetrable mystique, but once it has been sampled it becomes an instant success with its fresh taste. This dish can be cooked well in advance and will wait happily at a mezze table.

900 g/2 lb. fresh okra

150 ml/2/3 cup extra virgin olive oil

1 large onion, sliced

1 tsp ground coriander

1/2 tsp ground allspice

700 g/1¾ lb. fresh tomatoes, sliced, or a 400-g/14-oz. can tomatoes

2 dried limes (optional)

1/2 tsp sugar

2 tbsp finely chopped coriander/cilantro

salt and black pepper

SERVES 6

To prepare the okra, pare the conical tops with a sharp knife (similar to peeling potatoes). Put in a bowl, cover with cold water briefly, then drain – handle with care.

Heat the oil in a wide saucepan, add the onion and sauté until light golden. Add the ground coriander and allspice, then when aromatic, add the tomatoes, dried limes (if using), sugar, salt and pepper. Cook for 10 minutes, pressing the limes with a spatula to extract their juices.

Add the okra and spread them evenly in the pan. Add enough hot water until they are almost immersed in the sauce. Cook gently for about 30 minutes – shake the pan occasionally but don't stir as okra is fragile.

Sprinkle the fresh coriander over the top and simmer for 5–10 minutes more.

Serve warm or at room temperature.

ROASTED BABY PEPPERS STUFFED WITH FETA

Stuffed peppers are perhaps the best known of the stuffed vegetables prepared for mezze. These baby peppers are stuffed with tangy feta.

500 g/1 lb. 2 oz. baby red, yellow and orange (bell) peppers

3 tbsp olive oil

300 g/10½ oz. feta, rinsed and drained

1–2 tsp finely chopped dried red chilli/chile or paprika

2–3 tsp dried oregano

1 tbsp runny honey

1–2 tbsp pine nuts

a few basil leaves, to serve (optional)

SERVES 4–6

Preheat the oven to 200°C (400°F) Gas 6.

Using a small sharp knife, cut the stalks off the peppers and take out the seeds. Rinse and drain the peppers and place them in a baking dish. Pour over 2 tablespoons of the oil and place them in the preheated oven for about 45 minutes, turning them over from time to time, until they have softened and are beginning to buckle.

Meanwhile, crumble the feta into a bowl and fold in the rest of the olive oil with the chilli and oregano.

Take the peppers out of the oven and let them cool a little until you can handle them. Using your fingers, carefully stuff the feta mixture into each pepper. Be careful not to overstuff them as the skin will split. Lightly squeeze the tips of the peppers together to prevent the feta from spilling out and pop them back into the preheated oven for 15 minutes.

Drizzle the honey over them and return them to the oven for 5–10 minutes. Meanwhile, tip the pine nuts into a small pan and dry-fry them for 1–2 minutes until golden brown. Sprinkle the pine nuts on top and serve with a few basil leaves, if liked.

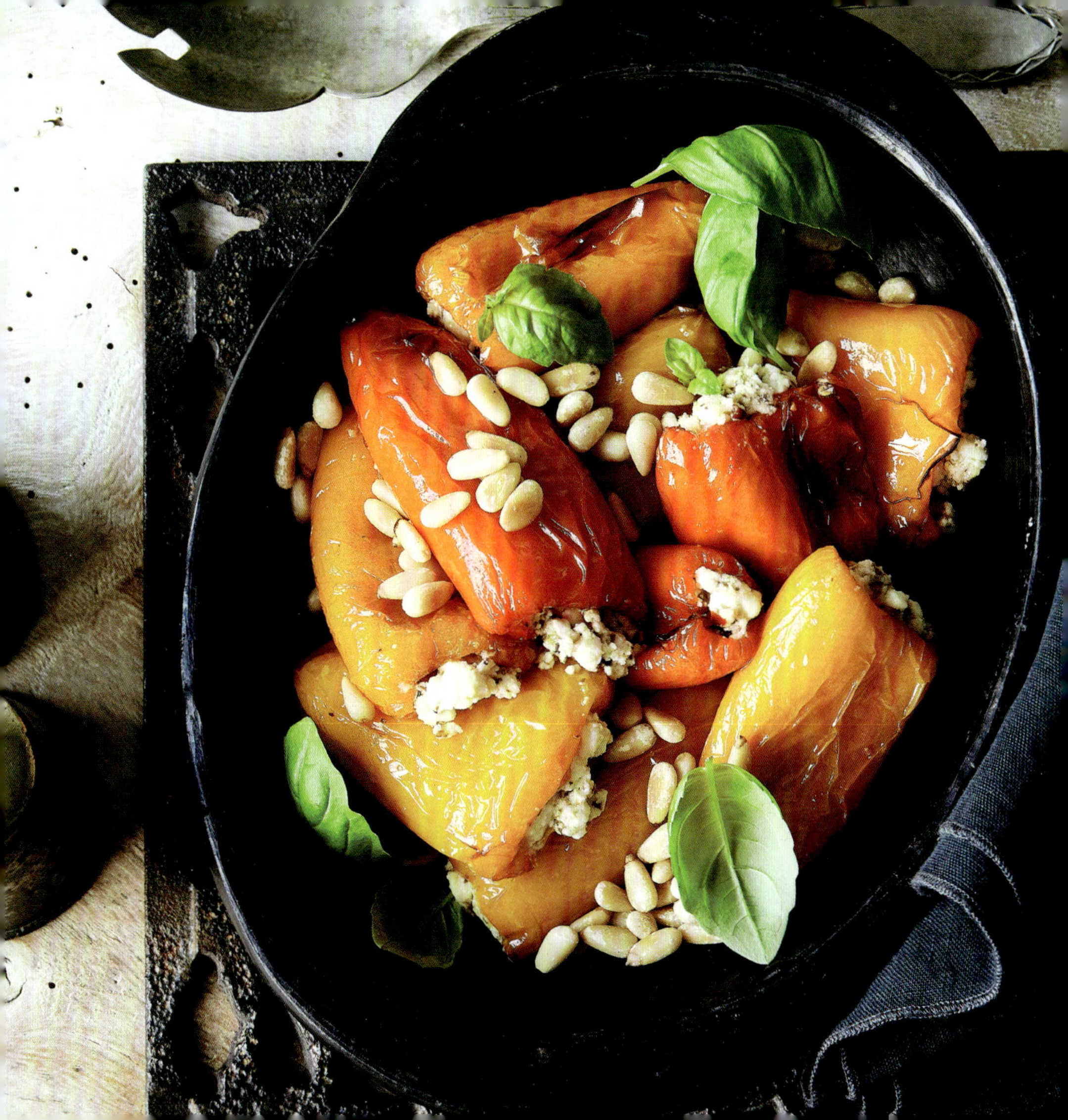

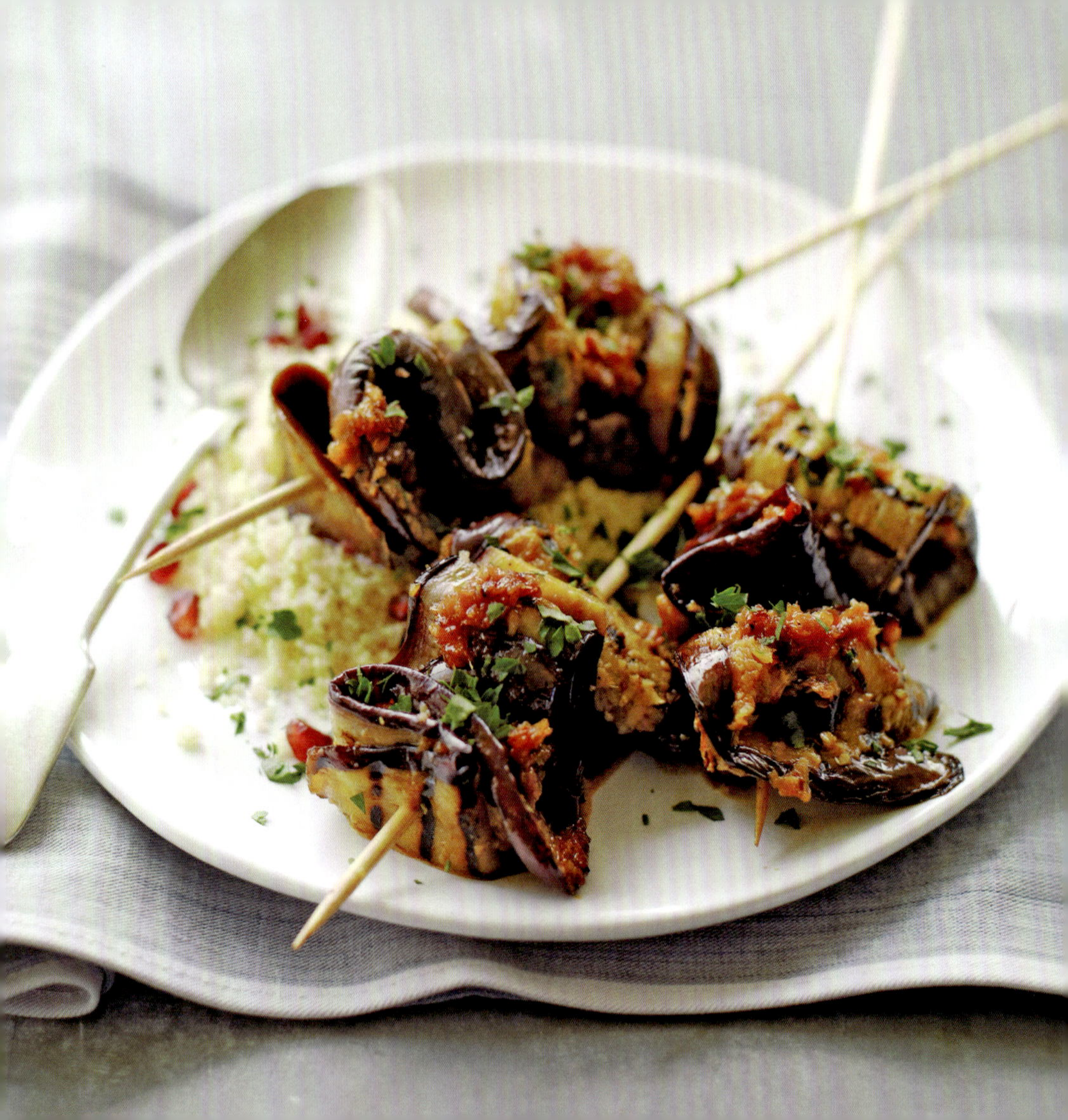

GRIDDLED AUBERGINE WITH HONEY & SPICES

For this delicious dish, you can either griddle or grill the aubergines/eggplants. Either way, the results make a delectable mezze mouthful.

Brush each aubergine slice with olive oil and cook them in a stove-top griddle/grill pan or grill them under a conventional grill/broiler, turning them over so that they are lightly browned.

In a wok or large heavy frying pan/skillet, fry the garlic in the olive oil, then stir in the ginger, cumin, harissa, honey and lemon juice. Add a little water to thin it, then place the aubergine slices in the liquid and cook gently for about 10 minutes until they have absorbed the sauce. Add more water if necessary and season to taste with salt.

Thread the aubergines onto the skewers, if using, and serve garnished with the parsley. Serve hot or at room temperature.

8 aubergines/eggplants, thickly sliced lengthways

1 tbsp olive oil, plus extra for brushing

2–3 garlic cloves, crushed

a thumb-sized piece of fresh ginger, peeled and crushed

1 tsp ground cumin

1 tsp harissa paste

5 tbsp runny honey

freshly squeezed juice of 1 lemon

salt

finely chopped flat-leaf parsley, to serve

4 metal or wooden skewers, to serve (optional)

SERVES 4

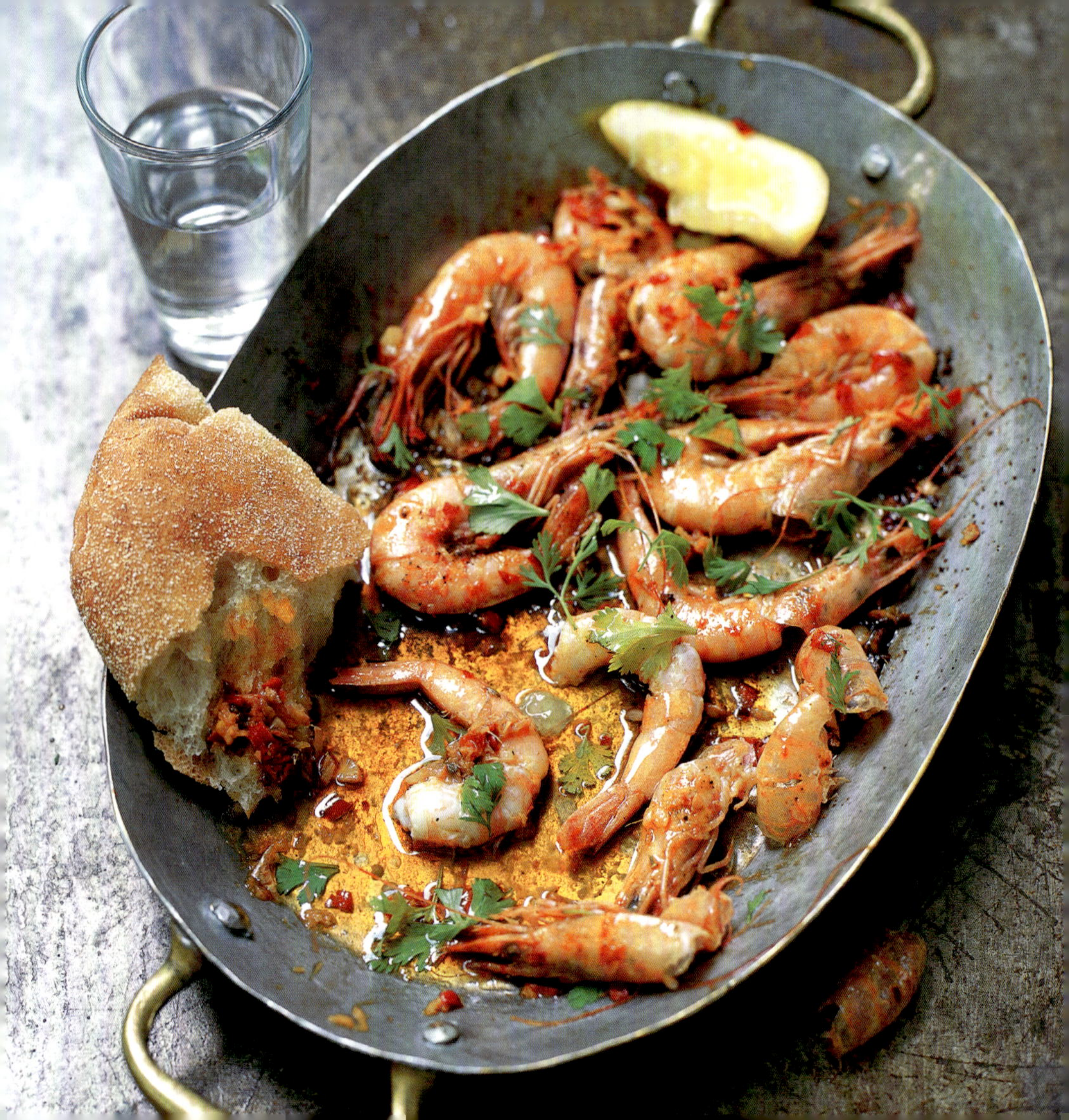

4
FISH & SEAFOOD

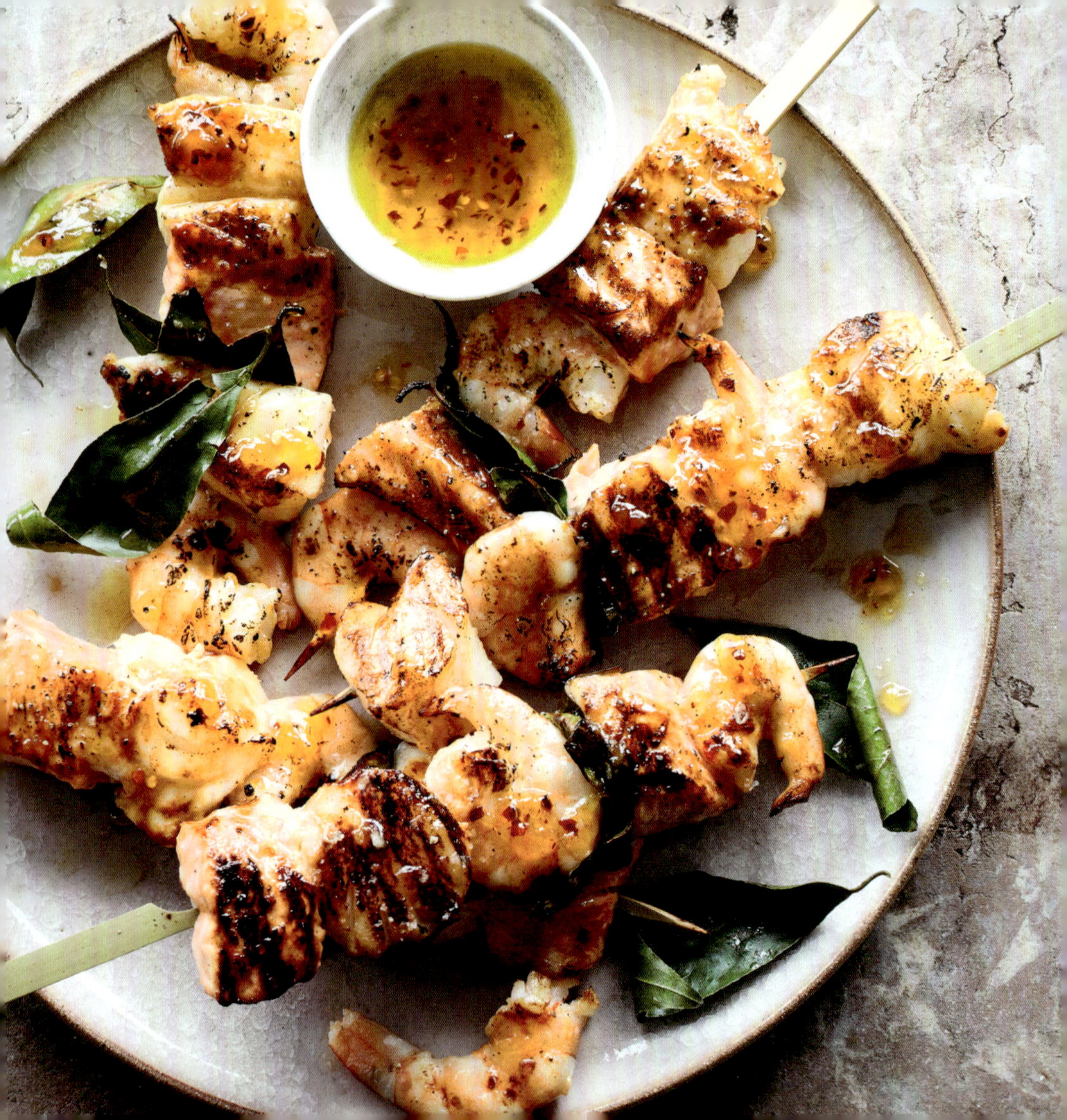

SEAFOOD SOUVLAKI WITH AN APRICOT GLAZE

4 tbsp apricot conserve

grated zest and freshly squeezed juice of 1 lemon

a handful of chopped dill

½ garlic clove, crushed

a 5-cm/2-inch piece of fresh ginger, grated

a pinch of dried chilli/hot red pepper flakes

1 tbsp olive oil

200 g/7 oz. skinless cod loin, cut into chunks

200 g/7 oz. skinless salmon, cut into chunks

12 raw king prawns/jumbo shrimp, peeled and deveined

12 fresh bay leaves

salt

4 wooden skewers, pre-soaked in water

MAKES 4

This combination of sweet, sharp apricots with the tangy zing of fresh ginger in this simple but effective glaze really complements the fish.

Preheat the grill/broiler until really hot.

In a large bowl, whisk together the apricot conserve (warmed if thick, just to loosen it), lemon zest and juice, dill, garlic, ginger, chilli flakes, olive oil and a pinch of salt. Once combined, decant one-third of the glaze into a small bowl to use later on.

Add the fish chunks and prawns to the large bowl with the glaze and toss it all until well coated. Thread the fish chunks, prawns and bay leaves onto the skewers.

Place the skewers under the preheated grill and cook for about 3 minutes, or until they start to caramelize, then turn once to cook the other side. The prawns will turn pink when they are cooked.

Just before the end of the cooking time, use a pastry brush to smother them with the reserved glaze.

FISH & SEAFOOD

DEEP-FRIED SQUID & POTATOES WITH GARLIC MAYONNAISE

This is inspired by the catch of the day on the Mediterranean coast.

4 Desiree potatoes, skin on, cut into 3-cm/1¼-inch pieces

400 ml/1¾ cups olive oil

10 sprigs of flat-leaf parsley

300 g/10½ oz. squid (about 6), cleaned and cut into 2-cm/¾-inch pieces

plain/all-purpose flour, seasoned with a few pinches of cayenne pepper, for dusting

salt and black pepper

lemon wedges, to serve

GARLIC MAYONNAISE

2 garlic cloves, peeled

100 g/3½ oz. mayonnaise

½ tsp Dijon mustard

pinch of cayenne pepper

1–2 tsp freshly squeezed lemon juice

SERVES 4

Cook the potatoes and garlic (for the mayonnaise) in boiling salted water until tender for about 15 minutes. Drain and spread on a baking sheet to steam and cool.

Mash the garlic and add to a bowl with the other garlic mayonnaise ingredients. Set aside.

Heat the oil in a deep frying pan/skillet over a medium-high heat. Add the potatoes, in batches and fry, turning occasionally, until golden. Remove with a slotted spoon and set aside on paper towels and keep warm. Add the parsley sprigs in batches and cook for 30 seconds until crispy, being careful not to burn them. Remove with a slotted spoon.

Dust the squid in the seasoned flour, shaking off any excess. Fry in batches in the same pan as the potatoes for 2–3 minutes until golden, then drain on paper towels.

Scatter the potatoes, squid and parsley on a serving platter. Season to taste and serve with lemon wedges and the garlic mayonnaise.

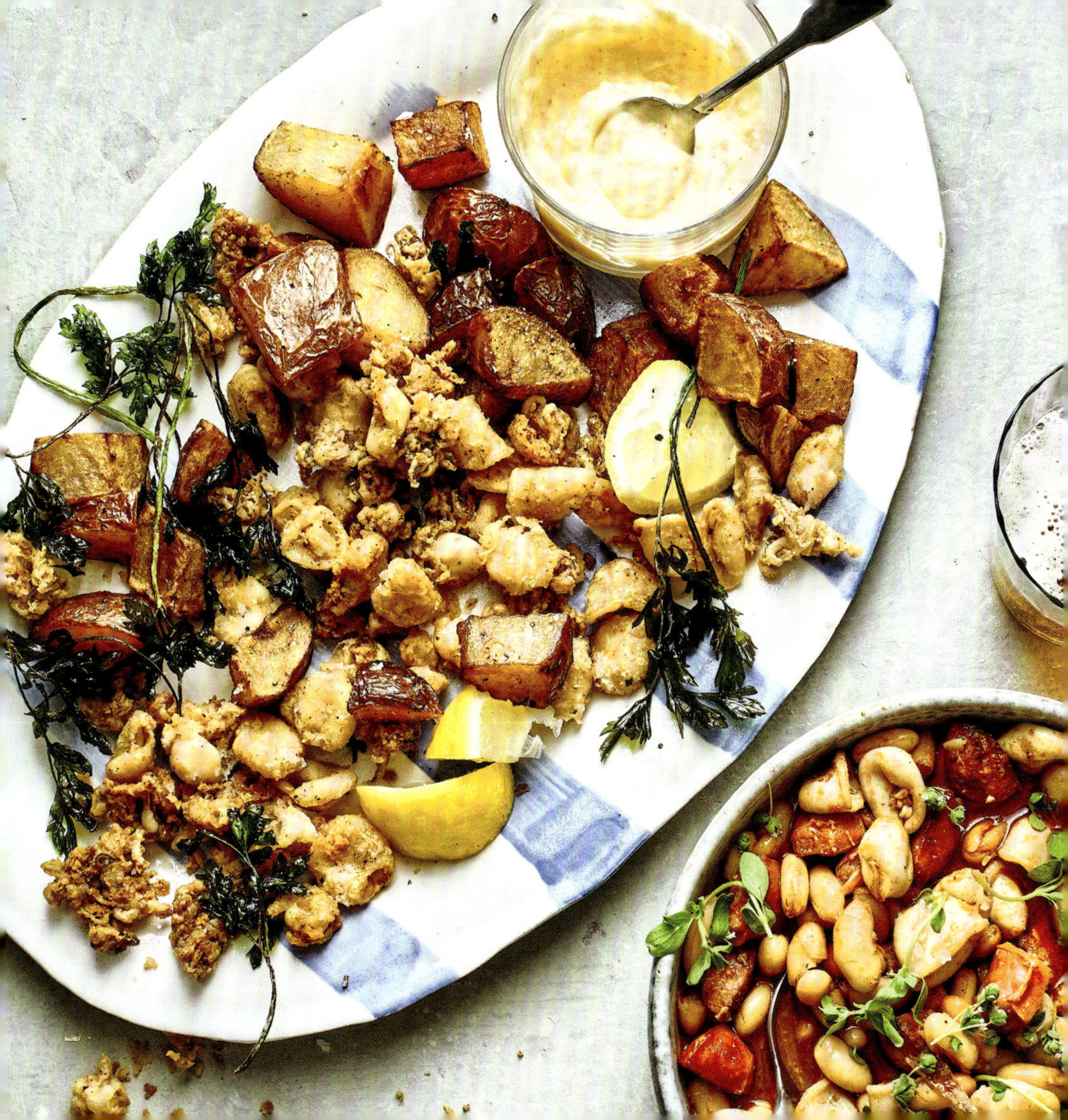

BRAISED BEANS, CHORIZO & CALAMARI

(see page 87, bottom right, for image)

- 2 tbsp extra virgin olive oil
- 1 chorizo ring, chopped into chunks
- 1 garlic clove, crushed
- 1 tsp smoked paprika
- 500 g/1 lb. 2 oz. squid, cleaned and cut into rounds
- 200 g/7 oz. cherry tomatoes, halved
- 4 tsp sherry
- 200 ml/1 scant cup vegetable stock
- 400-g/14-oz. can cannellini beans, drained
- 1 tbsp marjoram leaves
- 1 tbsp thyme leaves

SERVES 4

This is a winning dish that brings classic flavours and simple comforts together in a single bowl. Served alongside the Deep-fried Squid and Potatoes (see page 86) and some chunky bread, it makes for a lovely seafood lunch. Alternatively, it's great just eaten in a bowl on its own.

Heat the oil in a large frying pan/skillet over a high heat, add the chorizo, garlic and paprika and cook until the chorizo is crisp and the oil is coloured red. Remove the chorizo with a slotted spoon and set aside.

Return the pan to a high heat, add the squid and cook at a high temperature, stirring occasionally, for 4–5 minutes until it turns opaque and is just cooked through. Add the cherry tomatoes to the pan. Add the sherry and stir for 4–5 minutes until reduced. Add the vegetable stock and beans and return the chorizo to the pan. Cook, stirring, for about 8–10 minutes until combined.

Transfer to a platter, scatter with the marjoram and thyme leaves and serve immediately.

SQUID SALAD WITH TARRAGON & FRESH MINT

2 tbsp olive oil

2 garlic cloves, sliced

pinch of dried chilli/hot red pepper flakes

500 g/1 lb. 2 oz. squid, cleaned and scored

grated zest and juice of 1 lemon

200 g/7 oz. cherry tomatoes, quartered

1 tbsp capers

200 g/7 oz. green beans, blanched and refreshed in cold water

2 sprigs of tarragon, leaves picked

3 sprigs of mint, leaves picked

1 tbsp toasted almonds, chopped

salt and black pepper

SERVES 4

A juicy colourful summer salad that works well as part of a mezze meal or as a salad for a barbecue lunch. Very versatile, and great served with a crusty bread.

Gently heat the oil in a large frying pan/skillet over a medium heat. Add the sliced garlic and sauté gently, not to add colour, just to gently cook. Add the chilli flakes and some salt and pepper and sauté for about 3 minutes.

Raise the heat to high, add the squid to the pan and season again. Cook for a few minutes until just firm and opaque. Add the lemon zest and juice, tomatoes and capers and cook for a few more minutes, then take off the heat and leave to cool.

Once the mixture has cooled, place in a bowl and add all the remaining ingredients. This can be eaten just warm, at room temperature or chilled.

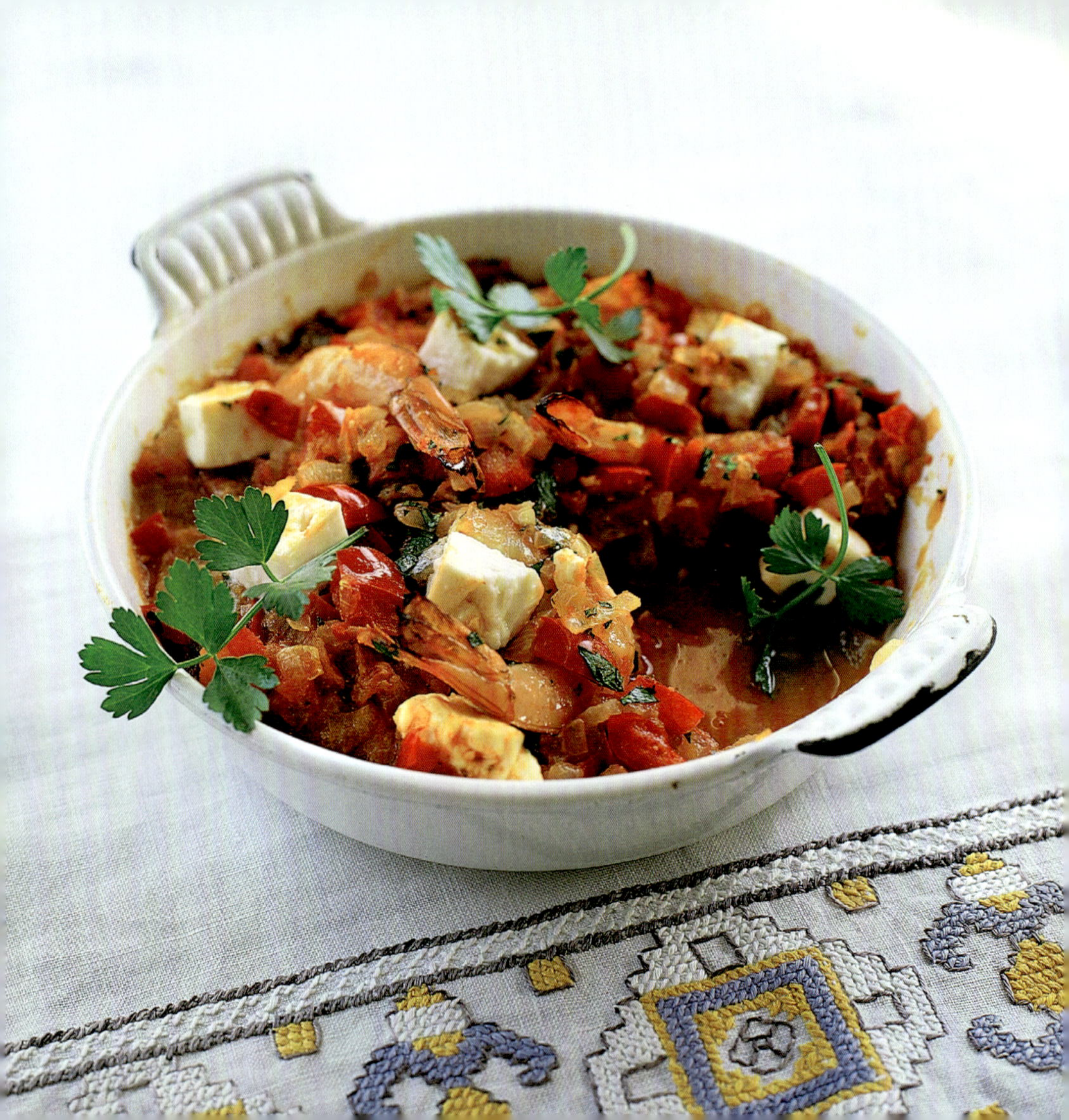

BAKED PRAWNS WITH TOMATOES & FETA

4 tbsp extra virgin olive oil

1 onion, finely chopped

1 red (bell) pepper, deseeded and chopped

500 g/1 lb. 2 oz. ripe tomatoes, blanched, peeled and coarsely chopped

a large pinch of sugar

½ tsp dried oregano

500 g/1 lb. 2 oz. raw tiger or king prawns/jumbo shrimp, peeled and deveined

3 tbsp finely chopped flat-leaf parsley, plus extra leaves to garnish

125 g/4 oz. feta, cut into cubes

salt and black pepper

SERVES 6

This is a Greek classic: sun-ripened tomatoes, tangy Greek feta, earthy oregano and fresh prawns/shrimp all baked to perfection.

Preheat the oven to 180°C (350°F) Gas 4.

Heat the olive oil in a frying pan/skillet, add the onion and sauté gently until translucent. Add the pepper and cook for 2–3 minutes more. Add the tomatoes, sugar, oregano, salt and pepper, and cook gently for 10–15 minutes until the sauce has thickened.

Add the prawns, parsley and half the cheese, then transfer to a small ovenproof dish and sprinkle the remaining cheese on top. Bake in the preheated oven for 30 minutes.

Serve hot or at room temperature, garnished with extra parsley leaves.

FRESH MUSSELS WITH SAFFRON & LEMON

This dish is enjoyed in *mezethopolia* (mezze restaurants) or outside on pavement tables in the old area of Lathathika city on Thessaloniki.

1.5 kg/3½ lb. live mussels, soaked in cold water

5 tbsp dry white wine

4–5 tbsp extra virgin olive oil

1 onion, finely chopped

1 garlic clove, chopped

1 green (bell) pepper, deseeded and chopped

freshly squeezed juice of ½ lemon

½ tsp Dijon mustard

a generous pinch of saffron threads, steeped in a little hot water

2 tbsp finely chopped flat-leaf parsley

black pepper

SERVES 4–6

Scrub the mussels well, knock off any barnacles and pull off the beards. Discard any broken mussels and any that won't close when they are tapped on the work surface. Rinse and drain in a colander.

Transfer to a large saucepan, add the wine and an equal amount of water, cover and cook over medium heat for 6–7 minutes, shaking the pan occasionally until they have opened. Remove with a slotted spoon into a colander resting in a bowl to catch their juices. If any remain shut at this stage, discard them too. Put the mussels on a plate and cover. Add any saved liquid to the saucepan and let it settle.

Heat the olive oil in a frying pan/skillet, add the onion and sauté until translucent. Add the garlic and pepper, and cook for 3–4 minutes. Add as much of the liquid from the mussels as you can, tilting the saucepan carefully in order to avoid any sediment. Alternatively, you can strain it through muslin/cheesecloth.

Add the lemon juice, mustard and saffron liquid, and boil gently for 15 minutes to reduce it. Add the mussels and a sprinkling of freshly ground black pepper, simmer for 5 minutes, sprinkle with parsley and serve hot.

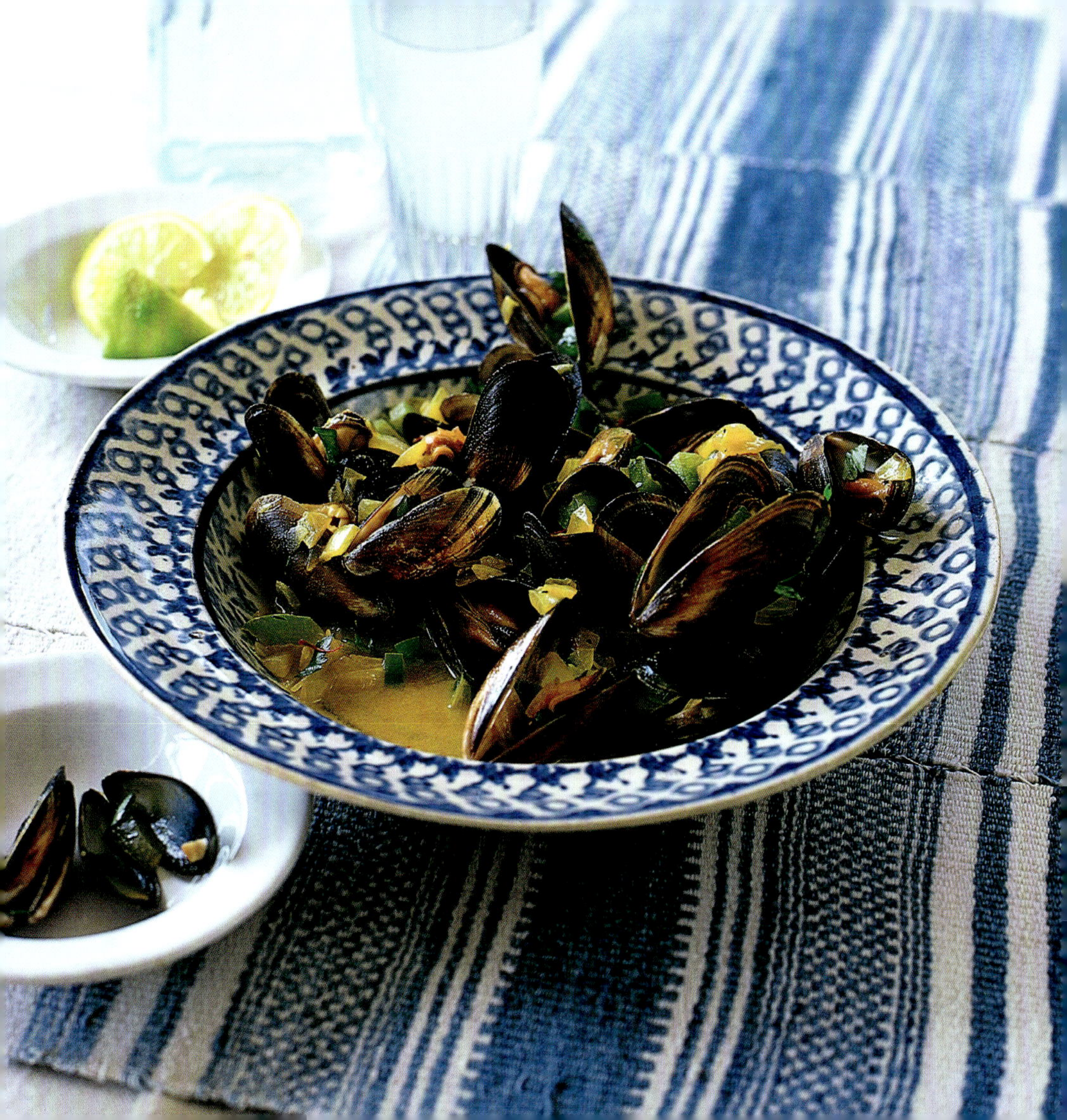

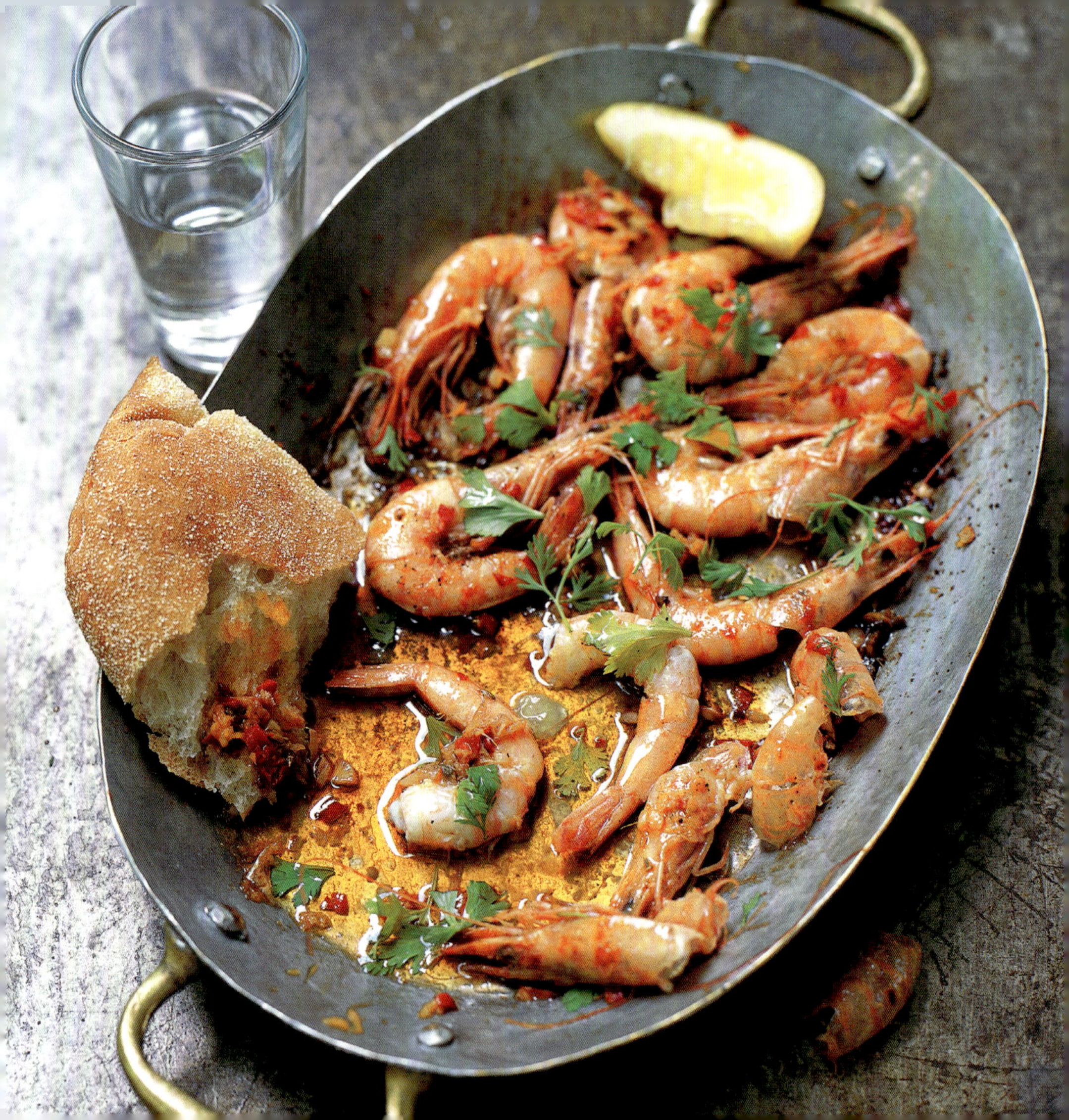

PAN-FRIED PRAWNS WITH GINGER, CUMIN & PAPRIKA

3 tbsp olive oil

2–3 garlic cloves, chopped

a 5-cm/2-inch piece of fresh ginger, peeled and grated

1 chilli/chile, deseeded and chopped

1 tsp cumin seeds

1 tsp paprika

500 g/1 lb. 2 oz. raw king prawns/jumbo shrimp in their shells

a bunch of coriander/cilantro, finely chopped

salt and black pepper

TO SERVE

lemon wedges

crusty bread

SERVES 4

This is a quick, easy way of preparing prawns/shrimp for a snack or mezze. Simply serve the juicy, piquant prawns straight from the cooking vessel with chunks of crusty bread to mop up the oil and spices left behind.

Heat the oil in the base of a tagine or a wide, heavy-based frying pan/skillet. Stir in the garlic, ginger, chilli and cumin seeds. As soon as a lovely aroma rises from the pan, add the paprika and toss in the prawns. Fry quickly over medium heat until the prawns are just cooked and have turned opaque. Season to taste with salt and pepper and sprinkle with the fresh coriander.

Serve the prawns immediately with the lemon wedges to squeeze over them and bread for mopping up the juices.

GRILLED TUNA KEBABS

600 g/1 lb. 5 oz. thick tuna steaks, cut into 5-cm/2-inch cubes

2–3 small red onions, quartered

2–3 mixed coloured (bell) peppers, deseeded and sliced into 8 pieces each

MARINADE

3 tbsp olive oil

freshly squeezed juice of 1 large lemon

2 garlic cloves, crushed

1 green chilli/chile, deseeded and finely chopped

1 tbsp dried oregano

1 tsp dried thyme

a handful of flat-leaf parsley, finely chopped

salt and black pepper

6 metal skewers

MAKES 6

Grilled fish is an integral part of Greek summer life and there is nothing more exhilarating than the aroma of barbecuing fish in the open air. These could be served with Tzatziki (see page 16).

To make the marinade, put the olive oil, lemon juice, garlic, chilli, oregano, thyme, parsley, salt and pepper in a large bowl and beat well. Add the tuna pieces and stir to coat. Cover with clingfilm/plastic wrap and chill in the refrigerator for 2–3 hours, stirring occasionally.

Separate the onion quarters into 2–3 pieces each, according to their size. Remove the tuna cubes from the marinade. Thread pieces of pepper, tuna and onion onto a skewer, finishing with a piece of pepper. Repeat with the remaining skewers to make six.

Grill over hot coals on a barbecue for 5–7 minutes on each side according to the strength of the fire, basting with the leftover marinade as they cook. Alternatively, cook under a preheated grill/broiler on all sides, about 10 cm/4 inches from the heat, for 6–8 minutes in total. Take care as tuna can become dry if overcooked.

Meanwhile, put the remaining marinade into a small saucepan and boil for 2–3 minutes. To serve, arrange the skewers on a platter and drizzle some of the leftover marinade over the top.

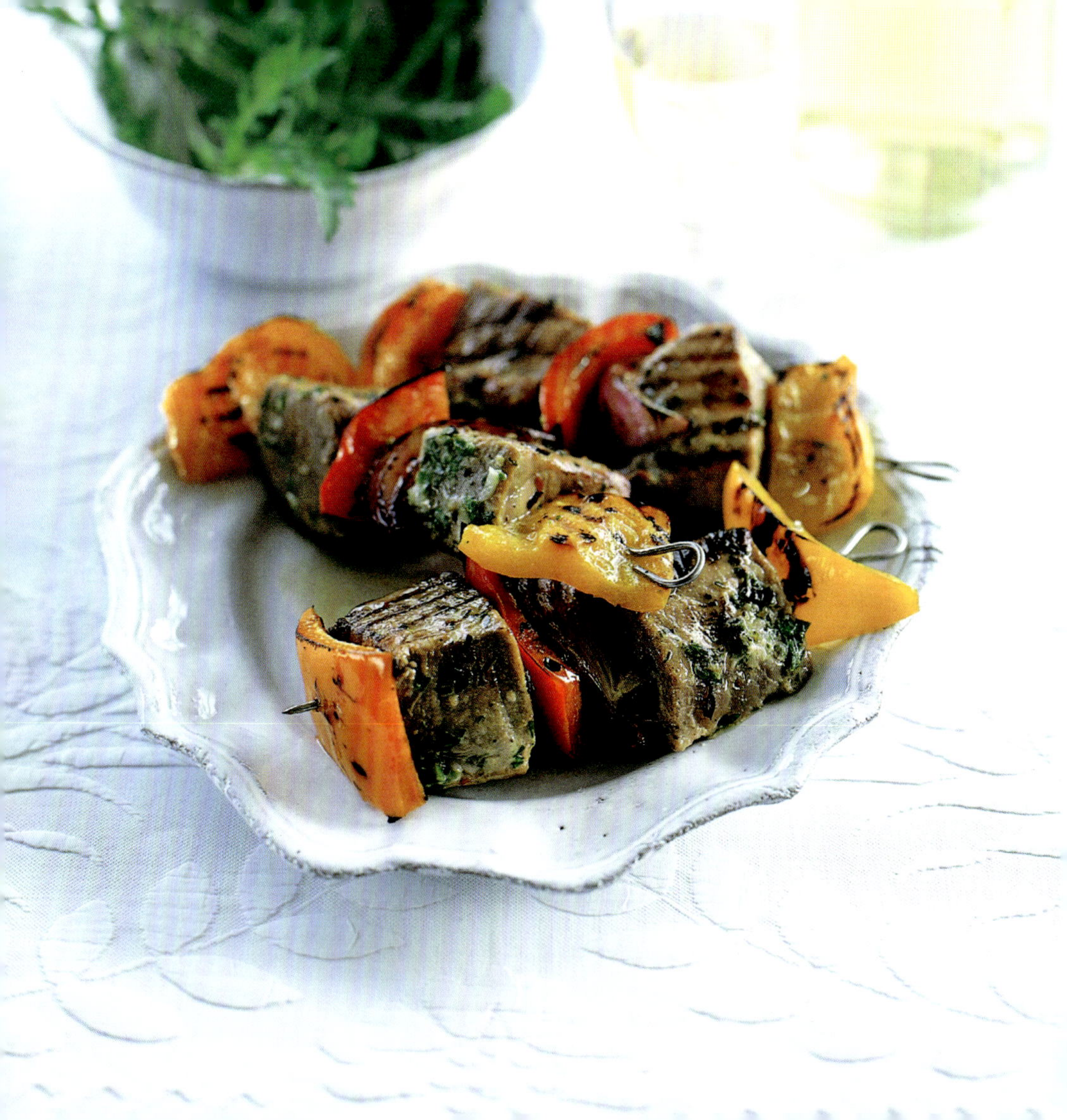

JEWELLED STUFFED SARDINES

16 fresh whole sardines, scaled and gutted by your fishmonger

40 g/scant ¼ cup raisins

3 tbsp white wine

80 g/1½ cups fresh breadcrumbs, made from a dry, stale loaf

a small pinch of sugar

a small handful of flat-leaf parsley leaves, chopped

finely grated zest of ½ orange

finely grated zest of 1 lemon

3 tbsp flaked/slivered almonds, lightly toasted

2 tbsp olive oil

lemon wedges, to serve

baking sheet, lightly oiled

SERVES 4

We should all eat more sardines. They're incredibly good for you, cheap and sustainable. Here, the stuffed fish is grilled until the skin is crisp and served with nothing more than a squeeze of lemon juice and a glass of wine.

First fillet the sardines. To do this, open out the gutted fish and place skin-side up on your work surface. Holding the tail with one hand, firmly press along the backbone with the other until the fish is completely flat. Turn the fish over and gently pull away the backbone. If the head is still attached, use scissors to snip where the backbone begins before you start. Keep pulling until you reach the tail end, then cut off the backbone and discard. Scrape away any remaining small bones. Cut each butterflied fish in half to make two fillets ready to stuff.

Preheat the oven to 240°C (475°F) Gas 9.

Put the raisins in a small heatproof bowl. Warm the wine in a small saucepan set over a low heat and pour it over the raisins. Leave them to steep; you want them to be nice and plump.

Toast the breadcrumbs in a dry frying pan/skillet for a few minutes until just crisp; you don't need to colour them. Remove from the heat and let cool in the pan for a minute before tipping into a mixing bowl. Add all the other ingredients, including the olive oil, and drain and stir in the raisins last. Mix to combine.

Lay a sardine fillet skin-side down on your work surface. Take a small amount of stuffing, about a heaped tablespoon, and gently press it together with your fingers to form a piece about the same size as the sardine and put this on the fillet. Lay another fillet flesh-side down on top of the stuffing and pat it down a little, to make a sardine sandwich, with the stuffing as the filling. Transfer to the baking sheet and repeat until all the sardines are stuffed.

Sprinkle over any unused stuffing and cook in the preheated oven for about 8 minutes, or until cooked through.

Lay the stuffed sardines on a platter and serve with lemon wedges for squeezing over.

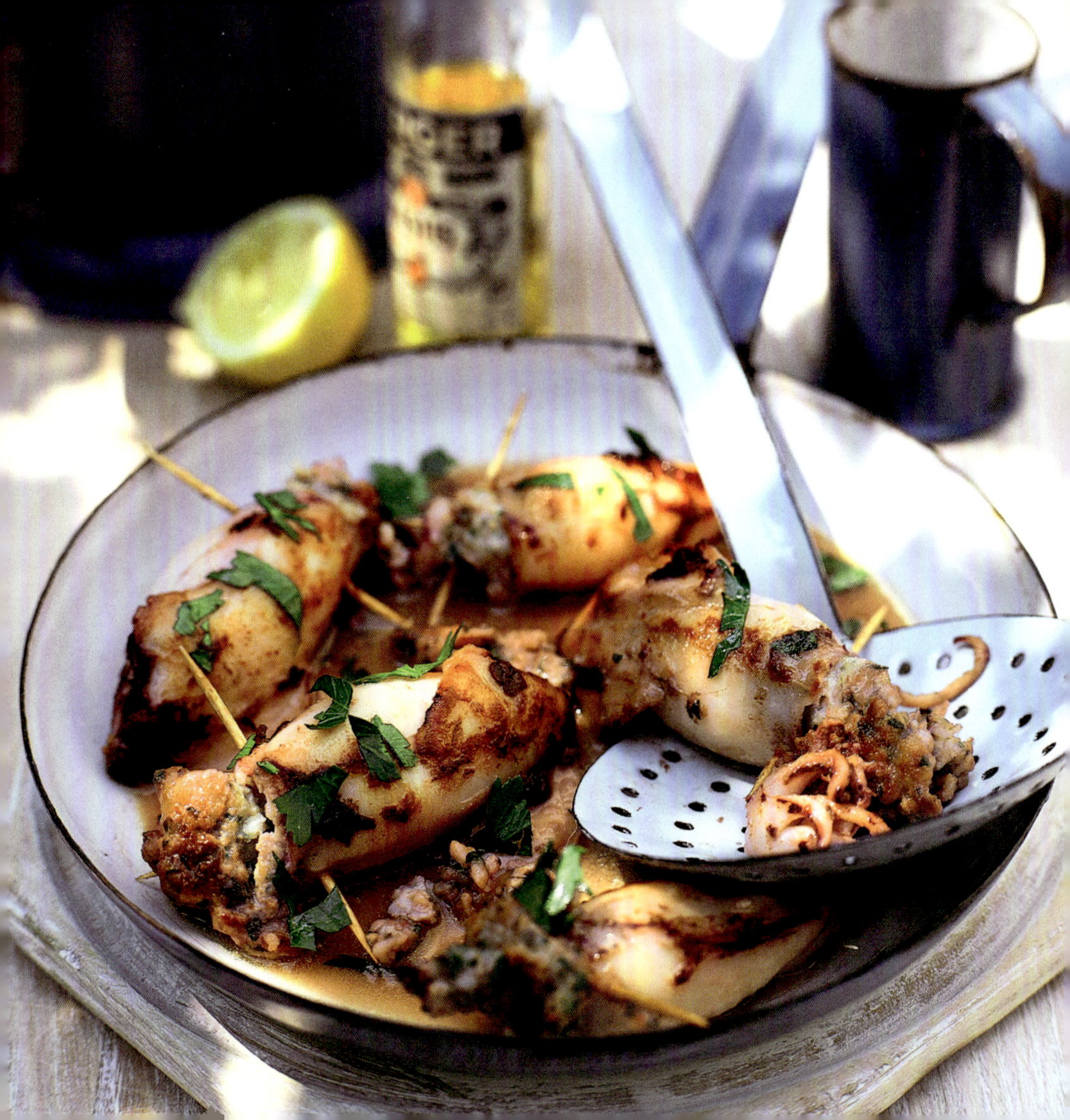

STUFFED SQUID

500 g/1 lb. 2 oz. squid, about 20 cm/8 inches long

350 g/12 oz. raw prawns/shrimp, peeled and chopped

a large handful of flat-leaf parsley, plus extra to serve

finely grated zest and freshly squeezed juice of 1 lemon

4 garlic cloves, thinly sliced

2 tbsp salted capers, rinsed and chopped

4 tbsp extra virgin olive oil

6 tbsp medium dry white wine

2 tbsp Pernod or Ricard

salt and black pepper

wooden cocktail sticks/toothpicks

SERVES 4

Squid crops up in every Mediterranean cuisine, prized as much for its simple, sweet, aniseedy taste as for its availability.

To prepare the squid, pull off and separate the tentacles from the body section. Trim off the tentacles whole, then discard the rest. Pull out and discard the transparent quill from each squid tube. Rinse the tubes.

To make the stuffing mixture, chop half the tentacles and mix with the prawns, parsley, zest and half the garlic. Stir in the capers, salt and pepper. Divide the mixture into 16 portions and push some stuffing inside each squid tube. Secure half with a wooden cocktail stick. Attach the remaining tentacle sections to the remaining tubes.

Heat the oil in a large frying pan/skillet. Add the remaining garlic and the stuffed squid and fry for 2–3 minutes. Pour in the lemon juice, wine and Pernod, then cover with a lid, reduce the heat and let simmer for a further 3–4 minutes, turning the squid once, until the filling is cooked (open one to check). Do not overcook or the squid will be tough. Serve hot with a trickle of sauce and extra parsley.

Note If you are unable to buy squid with tentacles, buy one extra tube and chop it to make the stuffing.

PRAWN & SCALLOP KEBABS

12 raw king prawns/jumbo shrimp, peeled to the tail

8 fresh scallops, shelled and thoroughly cleaned

8 cherry tomatoes

1 green (bell) pepper, cut into bite-sized squares

MARINADE

freshly squeezed juice of 2 lemons

4 garlic cloves, crushed

1 tsp ground cumin

1 tsp paprika

salt

TO SERVE

Skordalia (see page 68)

wooden skewers, pre-soaked in water

SERVES 4

This is one of the most popular ways to enjoy the jumbo prawns and scallops along the Mediterranean coast of Syria, Turkey and Lebanon.

To make the marinade, mix together the lemon juice, garlic, cumin, paprika and a little salt in a bowl. Rub the mixture into the prawns and scallops. Cover, refrigerate and leave to marinate for about 1 hour.

Thread the prawns and scallops onto the skewers, alternating with the tomatoes and green pepper, until all the ingredients are used up.

Prepare a charcoal barbecue or conventional grill/broiler. Cook the kebabs/kabobs for 2 minutes on each side, basting with any of the leftover marinade, until the prawn shells are orange, the scallops tender and the tomatoes and peppers lightly browned.

Serve hot with skordalia on the side for dipping.

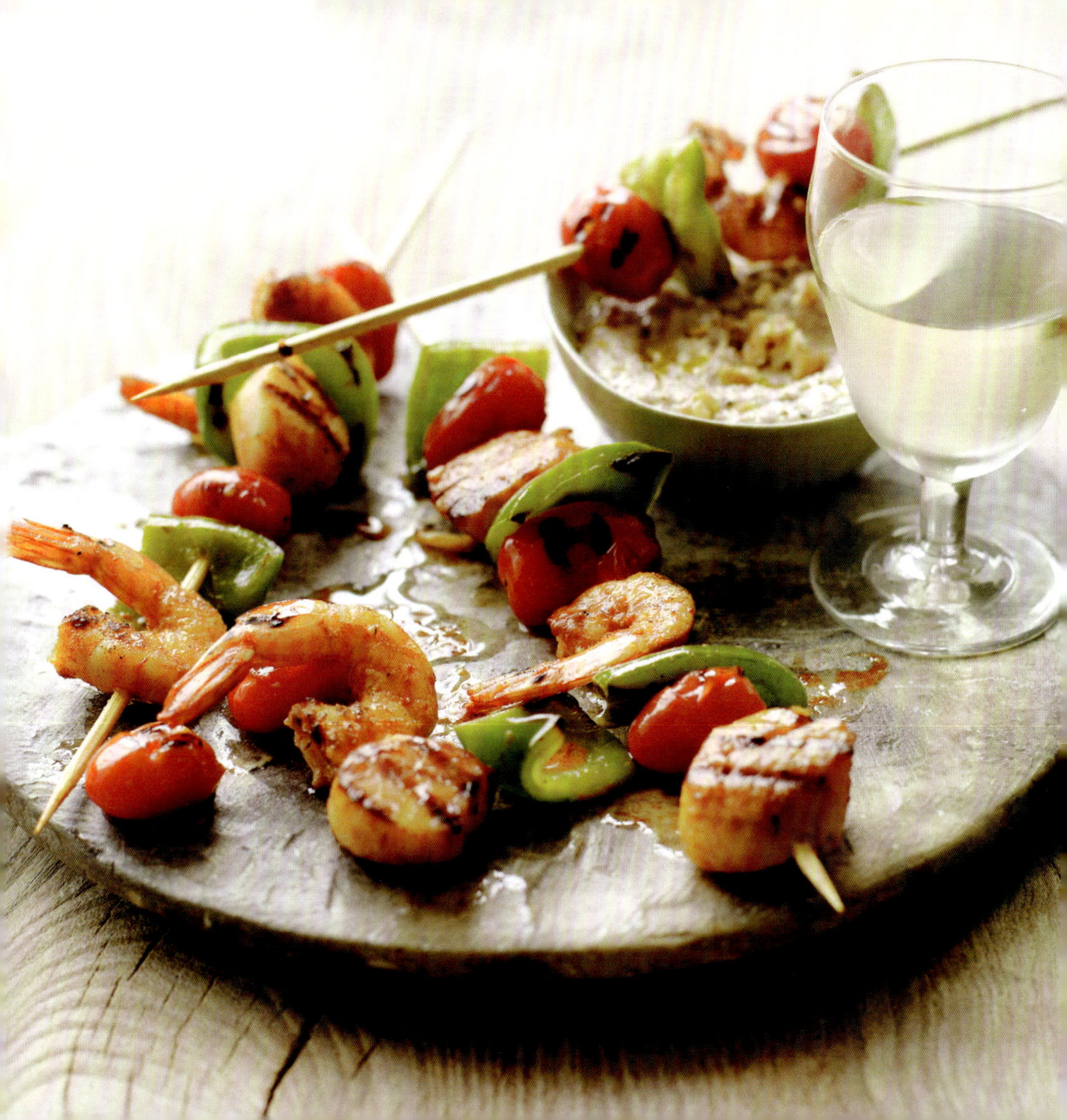

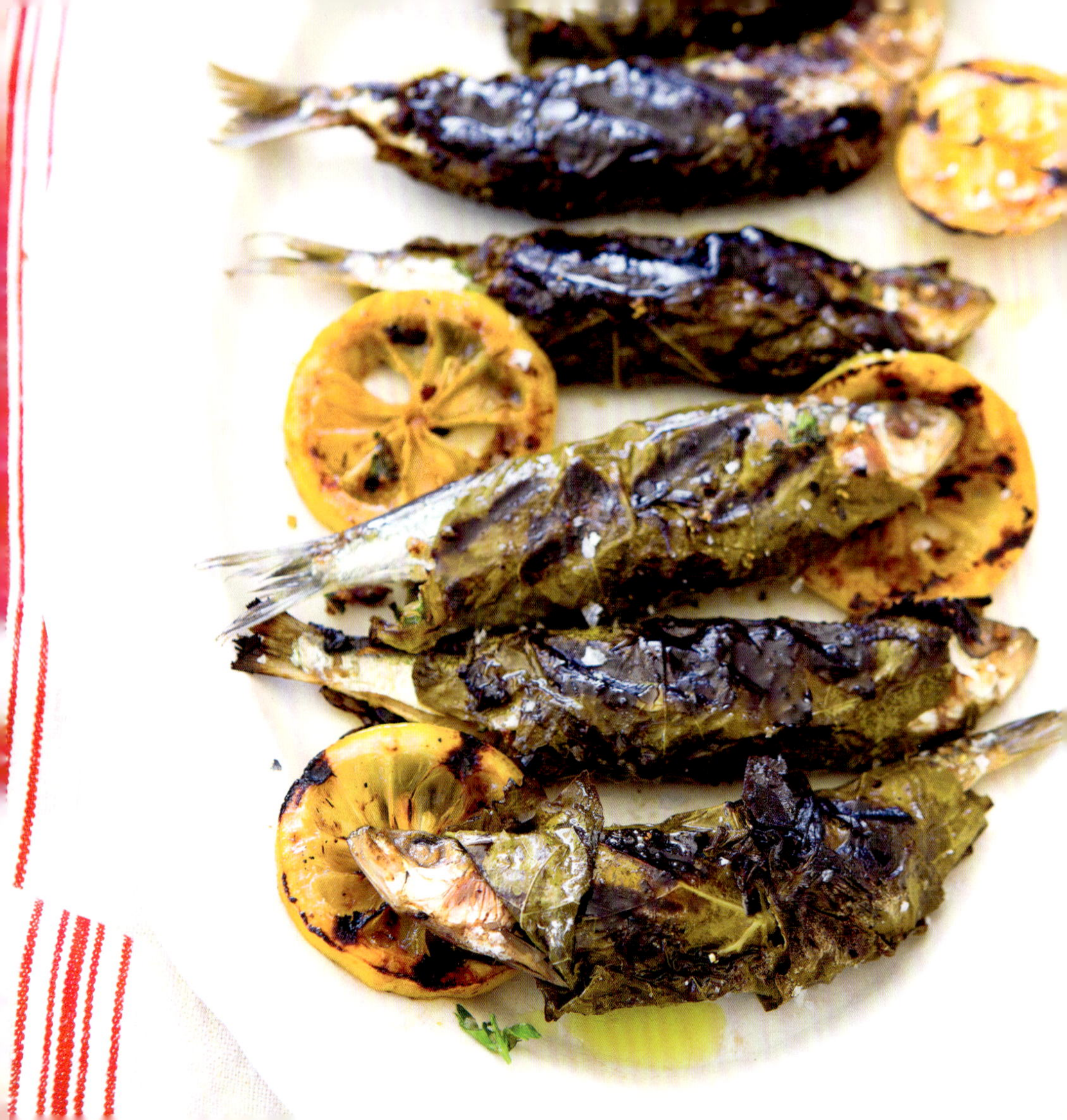

GRILLED VINE LEAF-WRAPPED SARDINES

This recipe evokes memories of holidays in Greece, especially long lazy lunches in wonderful little tavernas dotted along the beaches. At home it can be recreated under a hot grill, or you could even cook these on the barbecue, if you like.

12 sardines, gutted and cleaned

12 brined vine leaves

4 tbsp black olive tapenade

2 lemons, cut into thick slices

olive oil, for drizzling

salt and black pepper

SERVES 4

With a sharp knife, cut along the bottom of the sardines where they have been gutted. Rinse under cold water and pat dry with paper towels.

Lay the vine leaves down on a work surface with the stem facing upward. Place a sardine on each leaf, then stuff each of the sardines with a teaspoon of tapenade. Fold the stem end of the leaf over the fish and tuck in both sides, then roll up.

Preheat the grill/broiler to medium-high.

Grill/broil the sardines for 5 minutes, then turn them over and grill for a further 5 minutes until cooked. Lay the lemon slices on the grill and cook until charred.

Plate the sardines and grilled lemons, drizzle with olive oil, season with salt and pepper, and serve.

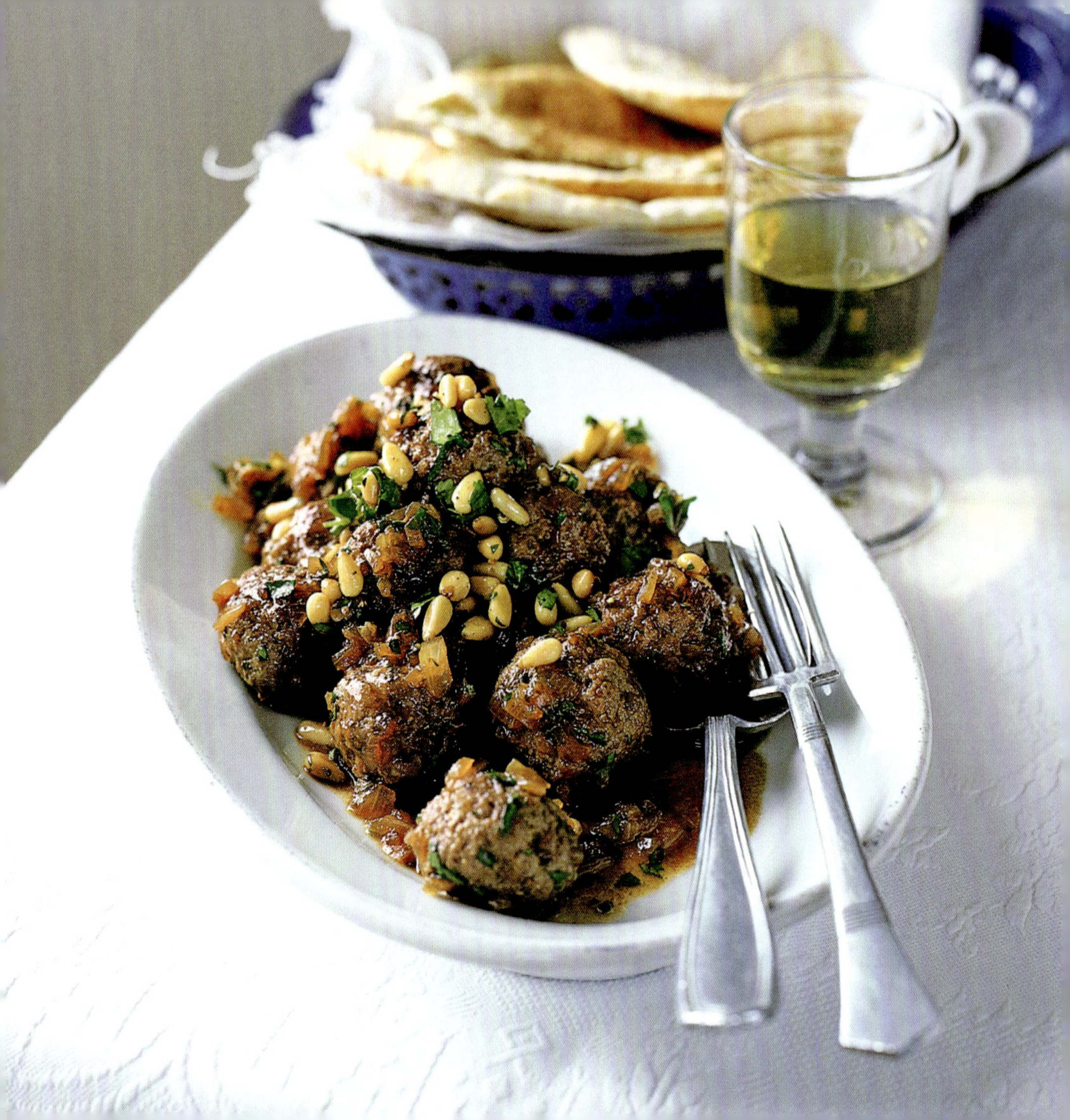

5
MEAT & POULTRY

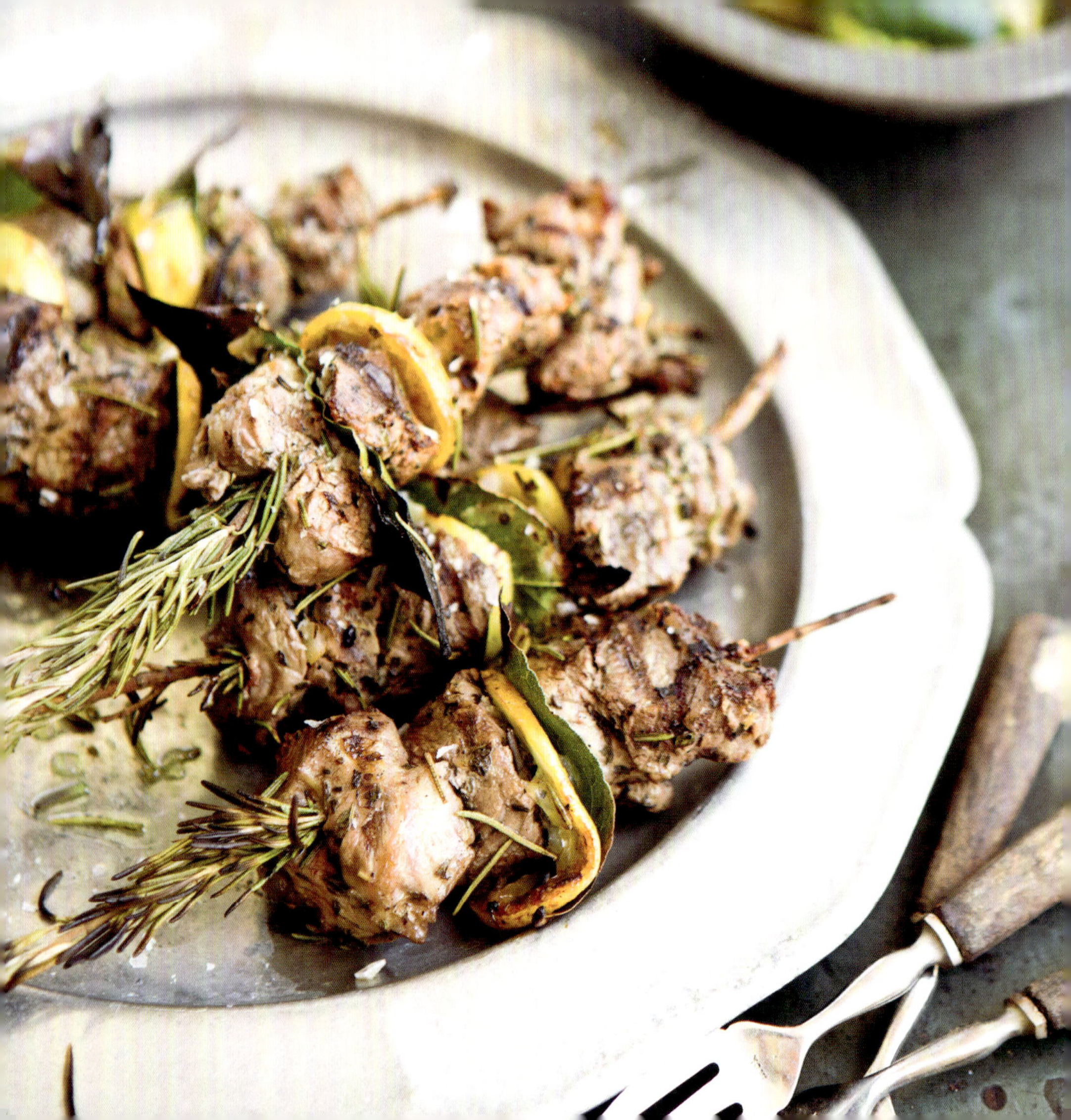

MINT & LEMON THYME LAMB KEBABS

Chargrilled meats and crunchy pickles are a great combo. If you have a rosemary bush in your garden, the branches make excellent skewers.

680 g/1½ lb. lamb shoulder

1 lemon

6 fresh bay leaves

salt and black pepper

MINT & LEMON THYME RUB

½ preserved lemon, finely chopped

1 tbsp dried mint

2 tbsp lemon thyme leaves

1 tbsp rosemary leaves

60 ml/¼ cup extra virgin olive oil

grated zest and freshly squeezed juice of 1 lemon

6 wooden skewers, pre-soaked in water, or rosemary branches

MAKES 6

For the rub, put all the ingredients in a bowl and mix together. Season to taste with salt and pepper. Set aside.

Rinse the lamb under cold running water and pat dry with paper towels. Cut the lamb into 3-cm/1¼-inch cubes and put in a mixing bowl. Sprinkle the rub over the lamb and toss to coat evenly. Season with black pepper. (The salt from the preserved lemon should be enough.) Cover and refrigerate for 8–24 hours.

Slice the lemon in half, then cut each half into half moons.

Remove the lamb from the fridge and, while still cold, thread onto the prepared skewers or rosemary branches, along with the bay leaves and lemon slices. Cover the skewers and allow to come to room temperature.

On a medium–high barbecue or grill/broiler, cook the lamb skewers for 5 minutes, then reduce the heat to medium and turn them over. Cook for 6–8 minutes more, turning frequently to make sure all the sides are brown and crispy. If you prefer your meat well done, continue to cook the skewers to your preference.

SPICY CHICKEN KEBABS

750 g/1¾ lb. boneless chicken, cut into large cubes

2 small red onions, quartered

2 red or yellow (bell) peppers, deseeded and sliced into 8 pieces each

MARINADE

4 tbsp olive oil

freshly squeezed juice of 1 lemon

3 garlic cloves, crushed

1 tsp ground cumin

½ tsp ground allspice

½ tsp ground sumac

salt and black pepper

TO SERVE

pitta breads

chopped flat-leaf parsley

6 metal skewers

MAKES 6

These skewers of glistening grilled chicken with enticing garlicky aromas are best served hot with Tarator (see page 16) or Tzatziki (see page 16), and salads, such as the Lebanese classic, Tabbouleh (see page 56) – its fresh herby aromas fuse deliciously with the spicy kebabs/kabobs.

To make the marinade, put all the ingredients in a large bowl and whisk well. Add the chicken cubes and turn to coat well. Cover and chill in the refrigerator for 6 hours or overnight.

Pull the onion quarters into layers of 2 or 3. Starting with a piece of chicken, thread pieces of chicken, onion and pepper onto a skewer, then repeat with the remaining skewers. Grill over hot coals on the barbecue for 8–10 minutes on each side until golden, turning frequently. Alternatively, cook under a preheated grill/broiler, about 10 cm/4 inches from the heat, for 12–15 minutes, turning frequently.

Serve with pitta breads and chopped parsley for people to make their own kebabs/kabobs by filling the pitta with grilled chicken, peppers, parsley and onions. Alternatively, lay the hot pittas on a platter, pull the chicken and vegetables off the skewers and scatter on top. Sprinkle with parsley and serve immediately.

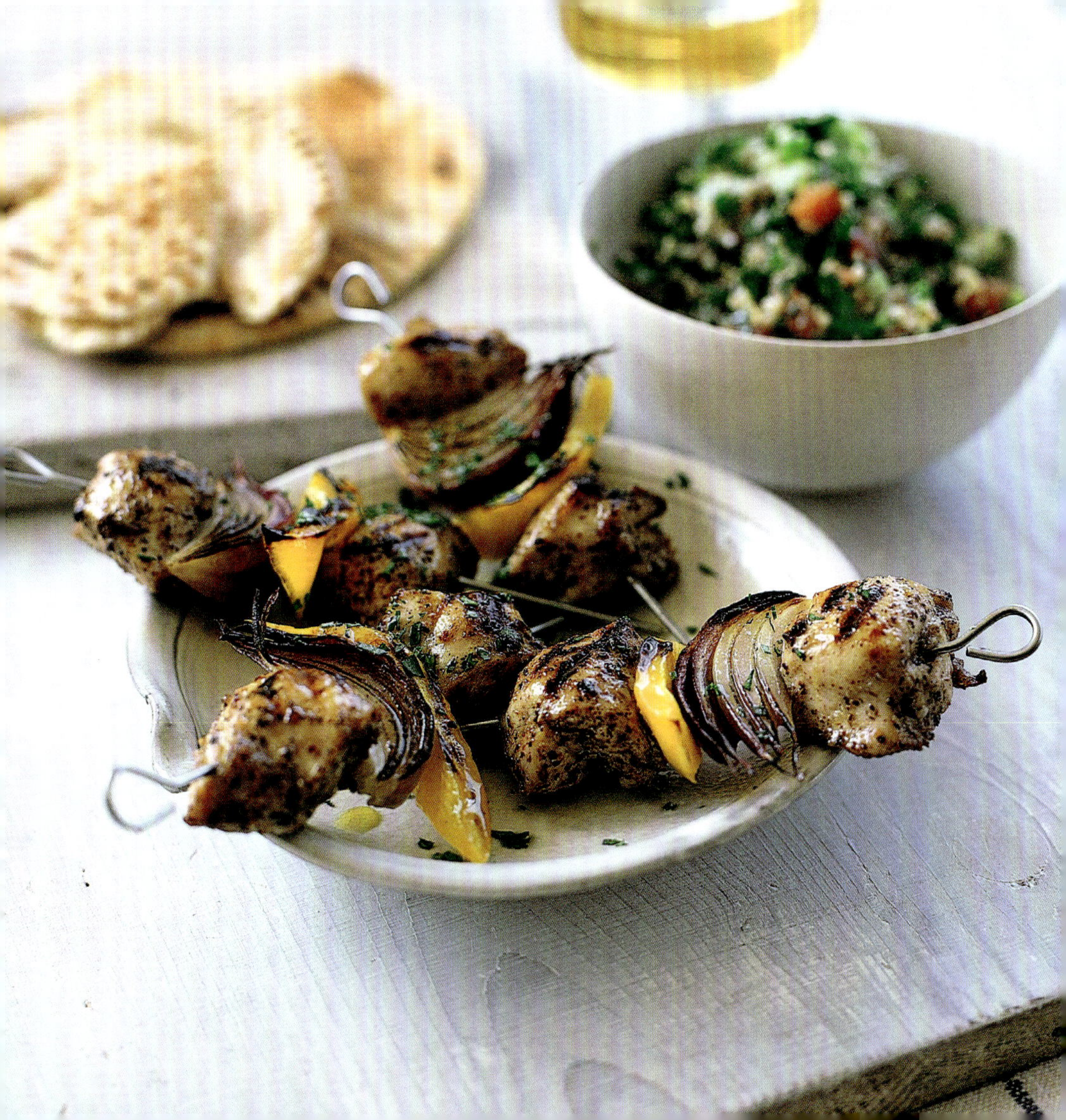

BAKED KIBBEH

Before food processors appeared, making kibbeh involved a lot of manual pounding, so it was mostly made for special occasions.

225 g/1½ cups fine bulgur wheat

1 large onion

500 g/1 lb. 2 oz. finely minced/ground beef or lamb

1 tsp ground allspice

1 tsp ground cinnamon

100 g/7 tbsp butter

salt and black pepper

STUFFING

3 tbsp olive oil

2 large onions, finely chopped

600 g/1 lb. 5 oz. minced/ground lamb

1 tsp ground allspice

1 tsp ground cinnamon

2 tbsp pomegranate syrup or freshly squeezed lemon juice

150 ml/⅔ cup hot water

3–4 tbsp pine nuts, toasted in a dry frying pan/skillet

4 tbsp chopped flat-leaf parsley

salt and black pepper

TO SERVE

Tzatziki (see page 16)

roasting pan (30 x 24 x 5 cm/12 x 10 x 2 inches), generously buttered

MAKES 12

To make the stuffing, heat the oil in a saucepan, add the onions and sauté until they start to turn golden. Increase the heat, add the meat and sauté until the moisture has evaporated and it starts to sizzle, 10–12 minutes.

Add the allspice and cinnamon and fry for 2–3 minutes. Add salt, pepper, the pomegranate syrup and water, cover and simmer for 30 minutes. Remove from the heat and stir in the pine nuts and chopped parsley. Set aside.

To make the kibbeh, soak the bulgur in a bowl of cold water for 10 minutes. Change the water once and soak for another 5 minutes. Drain.

Preheat the oven to 180°C (350°F) Gas 4.

Put the onion in a food processor and pulse until finely chopped. Add the minced lamb, allspice, cinnamon, salt and pepper. Process until smooth. Transfer to a bowl and add the drained bulgur.

Have a bowl of cold water with some ice cubes in it ready. Wet your hand in the cold water and knead the mixture for a few minutes. Divide the kibbeh mixture into two portions.

Dip your hands in the cold water, take a small handful from one of the kibbeh portions, flatten it between your palms and spread it neatly at the base of the roasting pan. Continue, wetting your hands and joining the pieces neatly and overlapping slightly until the whole base is covered to about 1 cm/½ inch thick.

Spread the stuffing evenly over the base. Use the remaining kibbeh mixture to cover the top in the same way as before, by stretching and patching like a patchwork quilt. Score the top with a sharp knife into diamond, rectangular or square serving portions.

Dot the butter over the top and bake in the preheated oven for 20–30 minutes. (Do not overcook or it will become very dry.)

Run a sharp knife around the edges, then cut the pieces carefully and lift individually onto a platter. Serve hot or at room temperature with tzatziki.

MEATBALLS WITH PINE NUTS
(see page 106 for image)

Delicate meatballs with a silky texture and exotic spicy aromas are the crown of Lebanese cuisine and irresistible on a mezze table.

1 large onion

750 g/1¾ lb. minced/ground beef, or a mixture of minced/ground lamb and beef

2 garlic cloves, crushed

1 egg, lightly beaten

1 tsp ground cumin

½ tsp ground allspice

a pinch of ground cinnamon

3 tbsp finely chopped coriander/cilantro

3 tbsp olive oil

salt and black pepper

THE SAUCE

90 ml/6 tbsp olive oil

1 large onion, finely chopped

1 tsp plain/all-purpose flour

½ tsp ground allspice

½ tsp ground coriander

2 tbsp pomegranate syrup or freshly squeezed juice of ½ lemon

200 ml/¾ cup hot water

salt and black pepper

TO SERVE

3 tbsp pine nuts, toasted in a dry frying pan/skillet

pitta bread

MAKES ABOUT 20

Put the onion in a food processor and pulse until coarsely chopped. Add the beef, garlic, egg, cumin, allspice, cinnamon, salt and pepper, and process until smooth. Add the coriander and pulse briefly. Transfer to a bowl. Shape the mixture into walnut-sized balls with your hands. Set aside.

Heat the oil in a frying pan/skillet, add the meatballs in batches and fry gently until brown all over.

For the sauce, heat the oil in a large pan, add the onion and sauté until translucent. Add the flour, allspice, ground coriander, salt and pepper, and stir for 2–3 minutes. Add the pomegranate syrup and water, cover and simmer for 10 minutes.

Add the meatballs and roll to coat them in the sauce. Cover and simmer for 10 minutes. Sprinkle with pine nuts and serve hot.

HARISSA & POMEGRANATE RACK OF LAMB

Lamb works so well with North African spices. Here, the spices of the harissa run wild with a hint of sweetness from the pomegranate molasses. The lamb rack is cut into double chops, which are then grilled.

2 whole racks of lamb

4 tbsp harissa paste

1 tbsp pomegranate molasses

1 pomegranate

SERVES 6

Rinse the lamb under cold water and pat dry with paper towels. Cut the racks into double chops and place in a baking dish.

In a small bowl, mix together the harissa paste and pomegranate molasses, and pour over the lamb. Rub into the meat, making sure it is well coated. Cover and refrigerate for 8–24 hours.

Remove the lamb from the fridge and stir to make sure all the sauce is on the meat. Allow the meat to come to room temperature.

Preheat a barbecue or grill/broiler to medium–high. Put the lamb, skin-side down, on the barbecue or grill and cook for 5 minutes, then flip over. Reduce the heat to medium and cook for another 6–8 minutes. Cook for longer if you prefer your lamb well done.

Cut the pomegranate in quarters, then patiently extract the jewel-like scarlet seeds.

Plate the chops and sprinkle with the fresh pomegranate seeds.

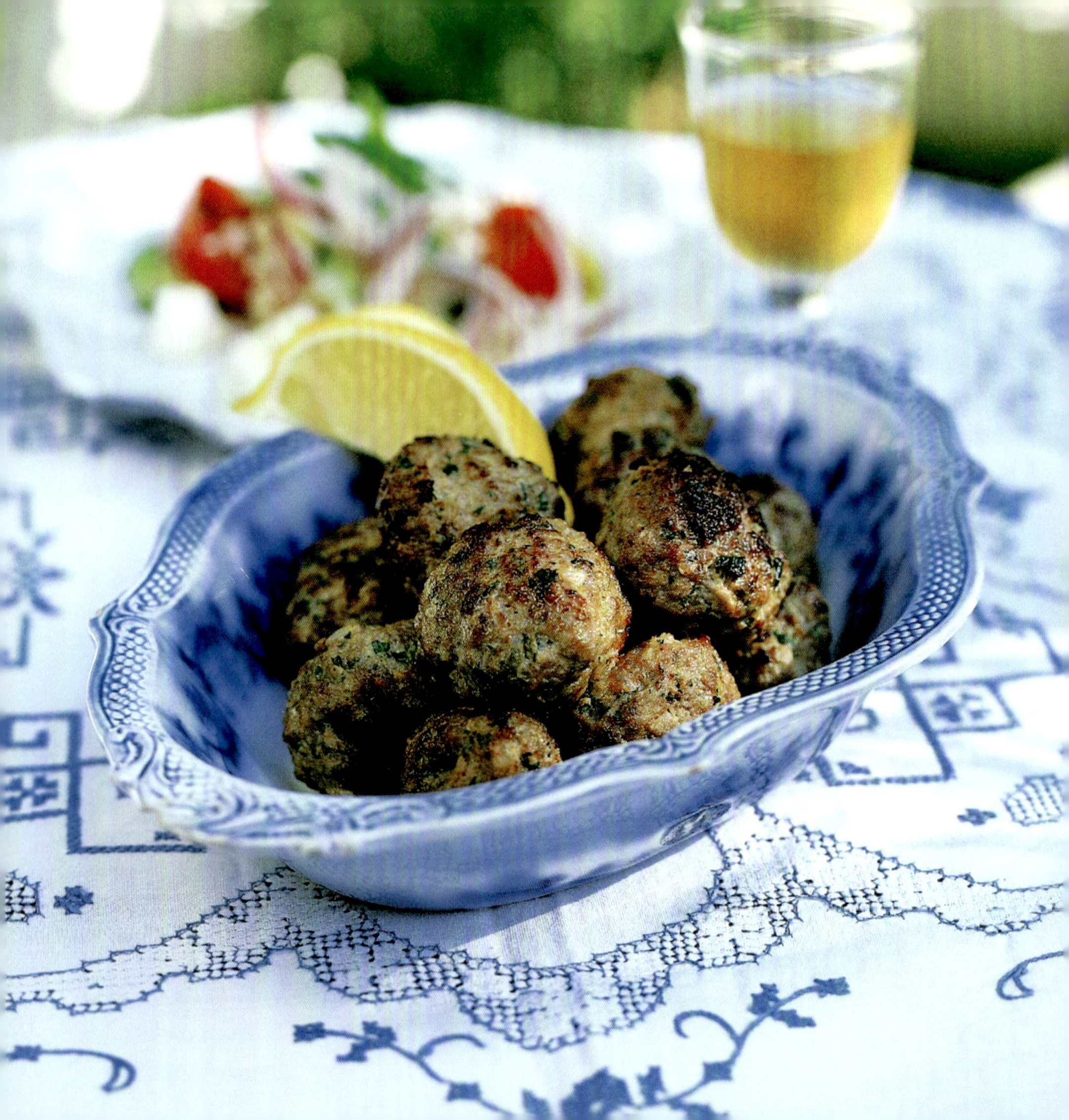

FRIED MEATBALLS (KEFTEDES)

3 medium slices of bread, crusts discarded, soaked in water

500 g/1 lb. 2 oz. minced/ground beef or lamb

1 tbsp freshly squeezed lemon juice or white wine

1 onion, grated

1 egg, lightly beaten

1 tbsp dried oregano

a small bunch of mint, chopped

5 tbsp plain/all-purpose flour

4–5 tbsp sunflower oil

salt and black pepper

lemon wedges, to serve

MAKES ABOUT 15

The delicious aroma of *keftedes* frying in the kitchen always brings a celebratory air with it. No social gathering in Greece is complete without them. Greek women pride themselves in shaping them into tiny, round, walnut-sized balls – the smaller the better – but of course you don't have to do that.

Drain the bread and squeeze out the excess water, then put the bread in a bowl. Add the minced beef, lemon juice, onion, egg, oregano, mint, salt and pepper. Mix it with your fingers until well amalgamated.

Put the flour on a work surface. Make round, walnut-sized balls of the mince mixture, then roll them lightly in the flour. For ordinary meals at home, you can make them bigger, then flatten them – this will make frying quicker.

Heat the oil in a non-stick frying pan/skillet, add the meatballs and fry, turning them around until golden on all sides. Remove and drain on paper towels, then serve immediately with lemon wedges.

PORK WITH QUINCES

If there was a beauty contest for fruit, quinces would be among the strongest contenders – and they taste wonderful with pork.

3 tbsp olive oil

6 boneless steaks of pork tenderloin (about 1 kg/ 2¼ lb.), or 6 leg steaks

freshly squeezed juice of 1 lemon

2–3 allspice berries (optional)

450 ml/2 cups hot water

2 quinces (about 750 g/ 1¾ lb.)

4–5 tbsp sunflower oil

2 tbsp demerara/raw sugar

¼ tsp ground cinnamon

salt

chopped flat-leaf parsley, to serve (optional)

SERVES 6

Heat the olive oil in a large saucepan over high heat, add the pork and fry until brown on both sides. Reduce the heat, pour half the lemon juice over the meat and let it evaporate for 2–3 minutes. Add the allspice berries, if using, and the hot water, cover and simmer for 30 minutes, adding a little salt towards the end.

Meanwhile, fill a large bowl with cold water and add the remaining lemon juice. Cut the quinces in quarters, then core and peel them. Put the quince quarters in the bowl of acidulated water straight away to stop them discolouring.

Drain the quinces and pat them dry. Slice each piece in half vertically. Heat the oil in a large frying pan/skillet. Working in batches, add as many of the quince slices as you can in one layer and fry slowly over gentle heat until golden. When they start to colour, turn each piece over and let them brown on the other side, 15–20 minutes. Spread on top of the pork.

Sprinkle with the sugar and cinnamon, and add a little more hot water until the quinces are almost covered. Tilt the saucepan to mix the ingredients. Cover and cook slowly for 45 minutes until tender. Do not stir after the quinces have been added, but lift and shake the saucepan gently instead. Serve hot, garnished with some fresh parsley, if liked.

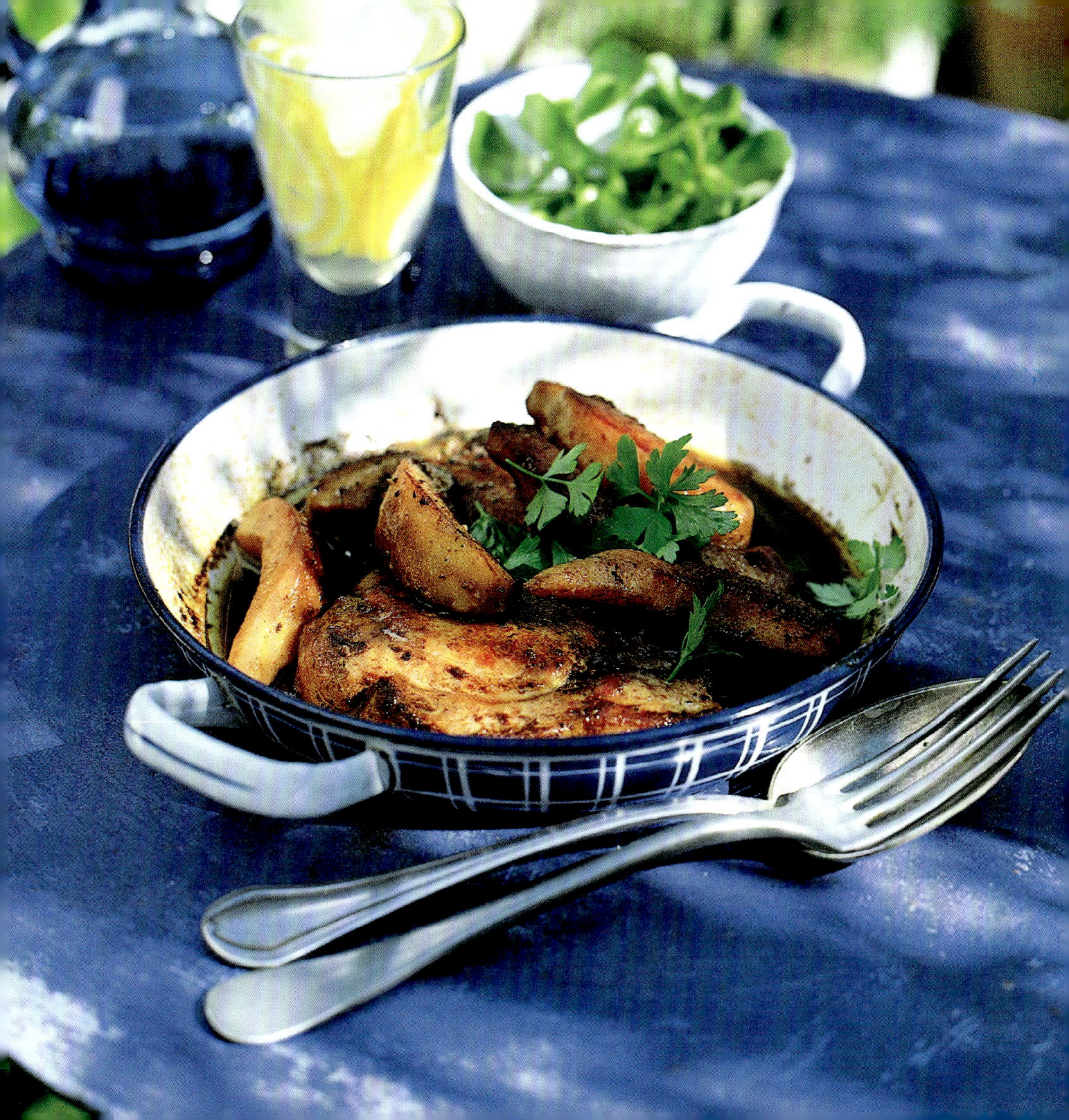

LAMB KOFTES WITH TAHINI YOGURT DIP

These spiced lamb skewers are more sophisticated than your average late night kebab/kabob, but just as tempting as mezze.

1 kg/2¼ lb. minced/ground lamb

1½ tsp ground cumin

1½ tsp smoked sweet paprika

1 tsp ground allspice

1 tsp chilli/chili powder

150 g/1 cup finely diced red onion (about 1 medium)

25 g/½ cup flat-leaf parsley, finely chopped

40 g/¾ cup coriander/cilantro, finely chopped, plus extra to serve

grated zest and freshly squeezed juice of 1 lemon

3 large/US extra-large eggs

1 tsp salt

60 ml/¼ cup sunflower oil, plus extra if needed

TAHINI YOGURT DIP

250 ml/1 cup Greek yogurt

2 tbsp tahini paste

2 tbsp freshly squeezed lemon juice

10 g/¼ cup mint, finely chopped

¼ cucumber, grated

1 garlic clove, crushed

½ tsp salt

TO SERVE

roughly chopped coriander/cilantro

lemon wedges

30 wooden skewers, pre-soaked in water

MAKES 30

To make the koftes, place all of the ingredients except the oil in a large mixing bowl and mix everything together using your hands.

Shape the kofte mixture around the soaked skewers (about 45 g/1½ oz. per skewer) in a sausage shape and press the mixture firmly together. Transfer to a baking sheet, cover with clingfilm/plastic wrap and set in the fridge for at least 2 hours, or preferably overnight, to firm up.

Preheat the oven to 180°C (350°F) Gas 4.

Heat the sunflower oil in a large frying pan/skillet set over a medium–high heat. Add the koftes in batches and cook for about 4 minutes, turning them until golden brown all over.

MEAT & POULTRY

Transfer to a clean baking sheet while you cook the remaining koftes in the same way, adding more oil to the pan each time if necessary.

When all the koftes have been fried, place them in the preheated oven for 5 minutes to cook through.

To make the dip, mix all the ingredients together and season with salt to taste.

Serve the koftes on a platter scattered with chopped coriander, with lemon wedges and the tahini yogurt dip on the side.

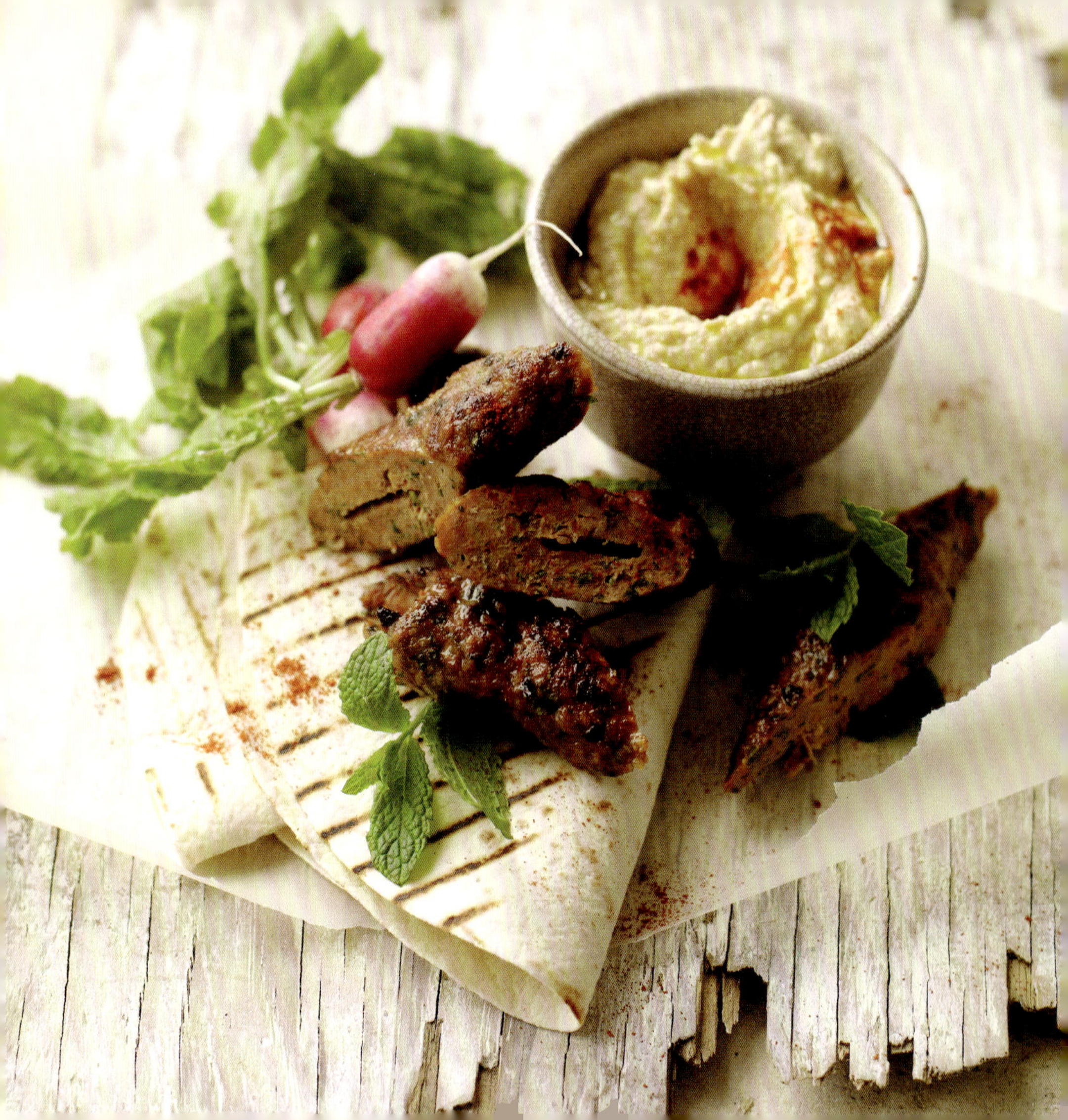

CUMIN-FLAVOURED LAMB KEBABS

500 g/1 lb. 2 oz. finely minced/ground lean lamb

1 onion, grated

2 tsp ground cumin

1 tsp ground coriander

1 tsp paprika

½–1 tsp cayenne pepper

1 tsp salt

a small bunch of flat-leaf parsley, finely chopped

a small bunch of coriander/cilantro, finely chopped

TO SERVE

hummus

a leafy herb salad

flatbreads

2 wide, flat metal skewers

SERVES 4–6

These kebabs are enjoyed throughout the Middle East and North Africa. You will need large metal skewers with wide, flat blades.

Mix the minced lamb with the other ingredients and knead well. Pound the meat to a smooth consistency in a large mortar and pestle, or whizz in a food processor. Leave to sit for an hour to let the flavours mingle.

Wet your hands to make the meat mixture easier to handle. Mould portions of the mix around the skewers, squeezing and flattening it, so it looks like the sheath to the sword.

Prepare a charcoal barbecue or preheat a grill/broiler. Cook the kebabs/kabobs for 4–5 minutes on each side.

When the kebabs are cooked through, slip the meat off the skewers, cut into bite-sized pieces and serve with hummus, a leafy herb salad and some flatbreads.

LEMON CHICKEN KEBABS

This Ottoman dish is impressive and tasty, and best served alongside a refreshing salad.

freshly squeezed juice of 2–3 lemons

2 garlic cloves, crushed

4–6 allspice berries, crushed

1 tbsp crushed dried sage leaves

8 boneless, skinless chicken thighs

4 aubergines/eggplants

1 tbsp butter

sunflower oil, for deep-frying

lemon wedges, to serve

4 metal skewers (optional)

an ovenproof dish, well greased

SERVES 4

In a shallow bowl, mix together the lemon juice, garlic, allspice berries and sage leaves. Toss the chicken thighs in the mixture, rolling them over in the juice. Let marinate for about 2 hours.

Slice the aubergines thinly lengthways, so that you have at least 16 long strips. Soak the strips in a bowl of cold salted water for about 30 minutes. Drain them and squeeze out the excess water. In a wok or frying pan/skillet, heat sufficient oil for deep-frying and fry the aubergine, in batches, until golden brown. Drain on paper towels.

Preheat the oven to 180°C (350°F) Gas 4.

On a board or plate, lay two aubergine strips, one over the other in a cross, then place a marinated chicken thigh in the middle. Pull the aubergine strips over the thigh to form a neat parcel. Place the parcel, seam-side down, in the grease ovenproof dish and repeat the process with the remaining thighs. Pour the rest of the marinade over the top and dab each parcel with butter.

Cover the dish with foil and cook in the preheated oven for 30 minutes. Remove the foil, baste the parcels with the cooking juices, and return to the oven for a further 10 minutes.

Serve immediately, threaded onto skewers to secure them (if using), with wedges of lemon on the side for squeezing.

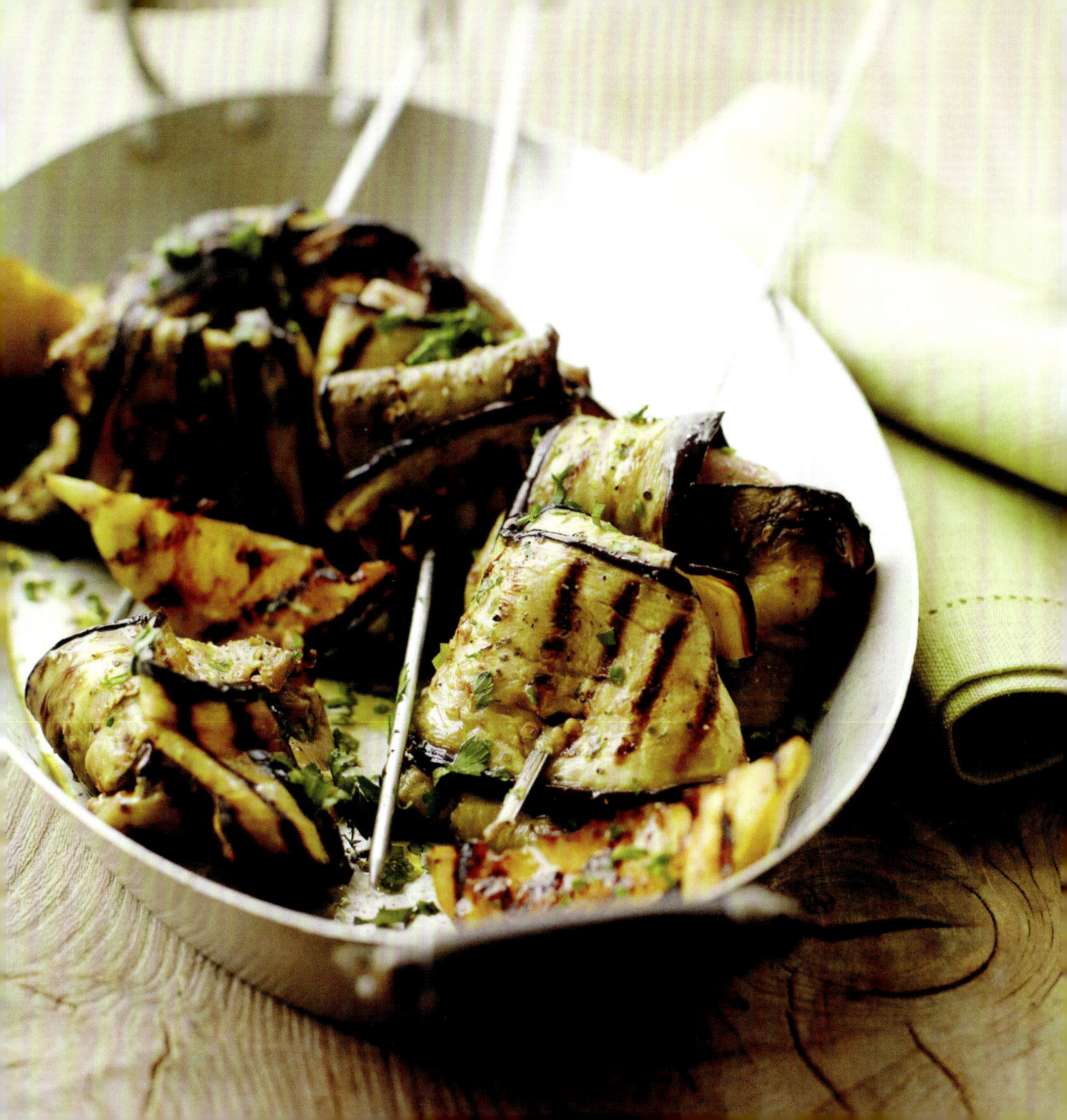

INDEX

aubergines/eggplants:
baba ghanoush 15
baked aubergines with garlic & tomatoes 72
lemon chicken kebabs wrapped in aubergine 124
pan-grilled aubergine with honey & spices 81

baba ghanoush 15
beans: braised beans, chorizo & calamari 88
beef: baked kibbeh 112–13
fried meatballs 117
meatballs with pine nuts 114
beetroot: roasted beetroot & carrots with walnut skordalia 68
breads: Moroccan country bread 49
yogurt pitta 51
broad/fava bean patties, spicy 41
bulghur (cracked wheat): baked kibbeh 112–13
Lebanese parsley salad 56
butter/lima beans: creamy butter bean dip 23
Greek gigantes plaki 67
butternut pies, spiced 35

cabbage salad 59
calamari, braised beans, chorizo & 88
carrots: roasted beetroot & carrots with walnut skordalia 68
celery & coconut salad with lime 60

cheese: baked prawns with tomatoes & feta cheese 91
bite-sized vegetable rolls with halloumi 64
cabbage salad with pomegranate 59
courgette, feta & herb patties 45
feta & chilli dip 22
feta baked in vine leaves with blistered tomatoes 29
fried cheese 30
roasted baby peppers stuffed with feta 78
spinach & cheese pie 36–7
tomato, cucumber, onion & feta salad 55
veggie halloumi souvlaki with harissa 71
whipped spicy honey feta 26
chicken: lemon chicken kebabs wrapped in aubergine 124
spicy chicken kebabs 110
chickpeas: hot houmous 123
roasted red pepper & chickpea hummus 12
spicy harissa falafel 42–3
chillies/chiles: feta & chilli dip 22
zhug 20
chorizo: braised beans, chorizo & calamari 88
coconut: celery & coconut salad with lime 60
cod roe: Lex's taramasalata 11
courgette/zucchini, feta & herb patties 45
creamy butter bean dip 23
cucumber: tomato,

cucumber, onion & feta salad 55
tzatziki 16, 25
cumin: cumin-flavoured lamb kebabs 123
pan-fried prawns with ginger, cumin & paprika 95

dips: baba ghanoush 15
creamy butter bean dip 23
feta & chilli dip 22
hot houmous 123
Lex's taramasalata 11
radish tzatziki 25
roasted red pepper & chickpea hummus 12
tahini yogurt dip 120–1
tarator 16
tzatziki 16, 25
yellow split pea purée 19
zhug 20
dolmades 74–5

falafel 41
spicy harissa falafel 42–3
fava 19
fennel seed & sea salt pita chips 48
filo pastry: spinach & cheese pie 36–7
fish: grilled tuna kebabs 96
grilled vine leaf wrapped sardines 105
jewelled stuffed sardines 98–9
seafood souvlaki 85

garlic: baked aubergines with garlic & tomatoes 72
garlic mayonnaise 86
tzatziki 16
zhug 20
Greek gigantes plaki 67

Greek-style rice with spinach, leek, dill & lemon 63
green beans: Provençal squid salad 89

harissa: harissa & pomegranate rack of lamb 115
spicy harissa falafel 42–3
veggie halloumi souvlaki with harissa 71
honey: pan-grilled aubergine with honey & spices 81
whipped spicy honey feta 26
hummus: hot houmous 123
roasted red pepper & chickpea hummus 12

jewelled stuffed sardines 98–9

kebabs: cumin-flavoured lamb kebabs 123
grilled tuna kebabs 96
lemon chicken kebabs wrapped in aubergine 124
mint & lemon thyme lamb kebabs 109
prawn & scallop kebabs 102
spicy chicken kebabs 110
keftedes 117
keftedes, tomato 46 112–13
kibbeh, baked
koftes, lamb 120–1

lamb: baked kibbeh 112–13
cumin-flavoured lamb kebabs 123

fried meatballs 117
harissa & pomegranate rack of lamb 115
lamb koftes 120–1
mint & lemon thyme lamb kebabs 109
spicy meat pastries 38–9
Lebanese parsley salad 56
leeks: Greek-style rice with spinach, leek, dill & lemon 63
lemons: fresh mussels with saffron & lemon 92
Greek-style rice with spinach, leek, dill & lemon 63
lemon chicken kebabs wrapped in aubergine 124
limes: celery & coconut salad with lime 60
okra with dried limes 77

mayonnaise, garlic 86
meatballs: fried meatballs 117
meatballs with pine nuts 114
Moroccan country bread 49
mussels: fresh mussels with saffron & lemon 92

okra with dried limes 77
onions: tomato, cucumber, onion & feta salad 55

parsley: Lebanese parsley salad 56
pastries, spicy meat 38–9
patties: courgette, feta & herb patties 45
spicy broad bean patties 41
peppers: grilled tuna kebabs 96
roasted baby peppers stuffed with feta 78
roasted red pepper & chickpea hummus 12
spicy chicken kebabs 110
pies: spiced butternut pies 35
spinach & cheese pie 36–7
pine nuts, meatballs with 114
pita breads: fennel seed & sea salt pita chips 48
yogurt pitta 51
pomegranate: cabbage salad with pomegranate 59
harissa & pomegranate rack of lamb 115
pomegranate salad with basil 60
pork with quinces 118
potatoes, deep-fried squid & 86
prawns/shrimp: baked prawns with tomatoes & feta cheese 91
pan-fried prawns with ginger, cumin & paprika 95
prawn & scallop kebabs 102
seafood souvlaki 85
stuffed squid 101

quinces, pork with 118

radish tzatziki 25
rice: Greek-style rice 63
stuffed vine leaves 74–5

saganaki 30
salads: cabbage salad with pomegranate 59
celery & coconut salad with lime 60
Lebanese parsley salad 56
pomegranate salad 60
Provençal squid salad 89
tomato, cucumber, onion & feta salad 55
sambusak 38–9
scallops: prawn & scallop kebabs 102
seafood 85–105
skordalia, walnut 68
souvlaki: seafood souvlaki 85
veggie halloumi souvlaki 71
spanakotyropitta 36–7
spiced butternut pies 35
spicy broad bean patties 41
spicy chicken kebabs 110
spicy harissa falafel 42–3
spicy meat pastries 38–9
spinach: Greek-style rice with spinach, leek, dill & lemon 63
spinach & cheese pie 36–7
squash: spiced butternut pies 35
squid: braised beans, chorizo & calamari 88
deep-fried squid & potatoes 86
squid salad 89
stuffed squid 101

tabbouleh 56
tahini yogurt dip 120–1
taramasalata 11
tarator 16
tomatoes: baked aubergines with garlic & tomatoes 72
baked prawns with tomatoes & feta cheese 91
feta baked in vine leaves with blistered tomatoes 29
Greek gigantes plaki 67
okra with dried limes 77
prawn & scallop kebabs 102
Provençal squid salad 89
tomato, cucumber, onion & feta salad 55
tomato keftedes 46
tyrohtipiti 22
tzatziki 16
radish tzatziki 25

vegetables: bite-sized vegetable rolls with halloumi 64
veggie halloumi souvlaki with harissa 71
vine leaves: feta baked in vine leaves with blistered tomatoes 29
grilled vine leaf wrapped sardines 105
stuffed vine leaves 74–5

walnut skordalia 68

yellow split pea purée 19
yogurt: tahini yogurt dip 120–1
tzatziki 16, 25
yogurt pitta 51

zhug 20

RECIPE CREDITS

Valerie Aikman-Smith
Harissa & Pomegranate Rack of Lamb
Mint & Lemon Thyme Lamb Kebabs
Vine Leaf Wrapped Sardines

Ghillie Başan
Courgette, Feta & Herb Patties
Cumin-flavoured Lamb Kebabs
Lemon Chicken Kebabs Wrapped in Aubergine
Moroccan Country Bread
Pan-grilled Aubergine with Honey & Spices
Paprika Prawns
Prawn & Scallop Skewers
Roasted Baby Peppers Stuffed Feta
Zhug

Clare Ferguson
Stuffed Squid

Tori Haschka
Tomato Keftedes

Kathy Kordalis
Braised Beans, Chorizo & Calamari
Deep-fried Squid & Potatoes
Feta Baked in Vine Leaves
Homemade Yogurt Pitta
Radish Tzatziki
Roasted Beetroot & Carrots with Walnut Skordalia
Squid Salad
Whipped Spicy Honey Feta

Theo A. Michaels
Creamy Butter Bean Dip
Fennel Seed & Sea Salt Pitta Chips
Greek Gigantes Plaki
Jewelled Stuffed Sardines
Roasted Red Pepper & Chickpea Hummus
Seafood Souvlaki
Spiced Butternut Pies
Spicy Harissa Falafel
Taramasalata
Veg & Halloumi Rolls
Veggie Halloumi Souvlaki

Shelagh Ryan
Lamb Koftes

Rena Salaman
Baba Ganoush
Baked Aubergines with Garlic & Tomatoes
Baked Kibbeh
Baked Prawns with Tomatoes & Feta
Cabbage Salad with Pomegranate
Celery & Coconut Salad with Lime
Feta & Chilli Dip
Fried Cheese (Saganaki)
Fried Meatballs
Grilled Tuna Kebabs
Meatballs with Pine Nuts
Mussels with Saffron & Lemon
Okra with Dried Limes
Pomegranate Salad with Basil
Pork with Quince
Spicy Broad Bean Patties (Falafel)
Spicy Chicken Kebabs
Spicy Meat Pastries
Spinach & Cheese Pie
Stuffed Vine Leaves
Tabbouleh
Tomato, Cucumber, Onion & Feta Salad
Tzatziki
Yellow Split Pea Purée

PHOTOGRAPHY CREDITS

Jan Baldwin
Pages 21, 44, 79.

Martin Brigdale
Page 100.

Peter Cassidy
Pages 14, 17, 18, 31, 37, 39, 40, 54, 57, 58, 61, 73, 75, 76, 82, 90, 93, 94, 97, 106, 111, 113, 116, 119.

Richard Jung
Page 52, 80, 103, 122, 125.

Mowie Kay
Pages 8, 10, 13, 24, 27, 28, 32, 34, 43, 50, 62, 64, 66, 69, 70, 84, 87, 99.

Erin Kunkel
Pages 104, 108.

Kate Whittaker
Page 121.

Isobel Wield
Page 47.